Lincoln Christian College

P9-DIG-032

Lincoln Christian College

FORESIGHT

**10 MAJOR TRENDS
THAT WILL DRAMATICALLY AFFECT THE FUTURE
OF CHRISTIANS AND THE CHURCH**

Howard A. Snyder
with
Daniel V. Runyon

Thomas Nelson Publishers
Nashville • Camden • New York

Copyright © 1986 by Howard Snyder

All rights reserved. Written permission must be secured from
the publisher to use or reproduce any part of this book, except
for brief quotations in critical reviews or articles.

Published in Nashville, Tennessee, by Thomas Nelson, Inc. and
distributed in Canada by Lawson Falle, Ltd., Cambridge, On-
tario.

Printed in the United States of America.

Unless otherwise noted, all Scripture quotations are from THE
NEW KING JAMES VERSION. Copyright © 1979, 1980,
1982, Thomas Nelson, Inc., Publishers.

Library of Congress Cataloging-in-Publication Data

Snyder, Howard A.
  Foresight.

    1. Christianity—20th century.   I. Runyon, Daniel V.
II. Title.
BR481.S65   1986   270.8'28   86-18025
ISBN 0-8407-5531-7

Bookstore

10'8

19 Jan 88

76718

To the new generation of Christian leaders emerging around the world

CONTENTS

INTRODUCTION:
Why Trace Trends?

We live in a quick-change society. This book alerts Christians to coming dramatic changes so that the church may equip itself for more effective ministry. We present ten trends which will shape the church and the world well past the year 2000.

How will these trends affect the church? What forces will shape it and society in general as we move into the twenty-first century? This book began with such questions. For answers, we surveyed over fifty knowledgeable people who hold a variety of perspectives. They are persons whose views and judgment we respect. Most are North Americans, but we also chose people with knowledge of, or significant experience with, the international scene.

Much has been written about trends that will affect the church. With few exceptions, it focuses so narrowly on North America that trends of greater scope are missed. In

fact, the most important current trend is the internationalization of the church and the accompanying shift in
the church's center of gravity. The church's dynamic center is moving from North Atlantic nations to the newer,
more vital churches of Latin America, Africa, and Asia.
Any discussion of trends that does not take this into account overlooks the currents which will have the greatest
impact on the church, both in North America and around
the world.

A trend is a direction or movement, a flow or general
tendency. Picture a river meandering back and forth,
sometimes flowing south, sometimes north, even though
the primary direction may be westward. Currents run
here and there, shaped by the landscape and obstacles in
the water. In spite of its roundabout course, the river
moves in one general direction. In the same way, a trend
is a direction or movement, a general tendency. To dis-
cern trends is to find out which way our society is moving.

A trend is more than an opinion. It is based on analysis
of what is actually happening, not something we only
think about or anticipate. And a trend is not a prediction.
The trend-watcher observes what is happening *now,* not
what will happen next year, or, to continue the river anal-
ogy, what will happen ten miles down the river. Change,
like a river, is not likely to reverse course; therefore, it is a
trend.

The study of trends should not be confused with identi-
fying truth. The biblical gospel remains our unchanging
foundation. The study of trends is simply a systematic
way of holding the Bible in one hand and the newspaper
in the other. It is a way of reflecting on what today's
world is and what tomorrow's world will be, and how we
may respond as Christians.

We used a threefold methodology to identify trends. First we surveyed over fifty observers of the church and society—educators, social scientists, church leaders, historians, theologians, and evangelists whom we regard as especially sensitive to emerging currents. That survey identified key trends and gave us a place to start.

Then we sent a follow-up survey to the original respondents as well as to other people. This one listed twenty-eight trends—the twelve most cited in the initial survey, plus sixteen suggested by those who had replied. Respondents identified and ranked what they thought were the ten most significant trends. In most cases the trends ranking highest in this survey have been given separate chapters in this book. (See Appendix I for copies of the surveys.)

Finally, we determined by research and interviews whether these trends were based on solid evidence. Where we have found such evidence, it is reported. Where evidence was inconclusive we either omitted the alleged trends or qualified our conclusions. We find the evidence convincing; readers can judge for themselves.

One influential book on trends has been John Naisbitt's *Megatrends: Ten New Directions Transforming Our Lives*. Because the trends traced and issues raised in *Megatrends* are significant for the church, we discuss Naisbitt's views in this book.

Naisbitt's megatrends are sometimes dismissed by critics as either blind prediction or mere opinion, but they are more. Naisbitt and his associates identify trends by studying the amount of space given to news stories in hundreds of small-city and regional newspapers throughout the United States. They especially watch news from "bellwether states," such as California, Florida, Washington, Colorado, and Connecticut, where important changes usually begin in this country. Through this method, buttressed by other research, Naisbitt documents changes in North American society.

This approach is not infallible. It is possible for trend-watchers to misinterpret the data, or to misjudge trends for other reasons. Still, any changes that modify the shape of society will inevitably affect the Christian church. It is helpful to examine how and why, and what this will mean for Christian faithfulness in coming decades.

For example, Naisbitt makes the startling claim that biology is replacing physics as the dominant metaphor of society.[1] He suggests that we are moving from the *machine* model to the *organic* model in understanding life and society. We are making the leap from seeing the world as a giant machine to seeing it as a living organism. This constitutes, in the terminology of philosopher Thomas Kuhn, a basic "paradigm shift" of considerable significance. If Naisbitt is correct, this shift has long-range implications for Christians now and in the early twenty-first century.

Naisbitt's megatrends are aimed mainly in the direction of the North American business scene, but to the degree that such trends signal long-term shifts in human society, they have deep meaning for the life and witness of the church. Consider, for example, the following four trends:

- From forced technology to high tech/high touch
- From national economy to world economy
- From centralization to decentralization
- From hierarchies to networking

These trends are vital matters for Christians, for they affect the way we feel, how we relate to technology, and the way we pattern our lives as individuals and groups.

Naisbitt suggests ten megatrends—ten "new directions" which are already beginning to shape our lives. In addition to the four listed above these include:

- From industrial society to information society
- From short-term to long-term thinking
- From institutional help to self-help
- From representative to participatory democracy
- From north to south—a demographic change
- From either/or to multiple choice[2]

Some of these trends have remarkable parallels in the church. In other instances Naisbitt's North American trends seem contrary to worldwide trends in the church. We will consider the significance of each trend for the church.

Theologian Jaroslav Pelikan begins his masterful book *Jesus through the Centuries* with the statement, "Regardless of what anyone may personally think or believe about him, Jesus of Nazareth has been the dominant figure in the history of Western culture for almost twenty centuries."[3] As we analyze trends, we will show that the influence of Jesus is growing in ways that will surprise many both inside and outside the Christian church. Jesus is becoming the dominant figure of global culture today. Yet, the witness among people who call themselves followers of Jesus is often compromised. We must examine this contradiction as well.

We are both pessimistic and optimistic about the trends shaping the world, and especially the church, over the next half-century. We believe the biblical perspective calls for pessimism about mere human effort producing a world of peace and justice, but for optimism about God's grace working through human agency and producing a substantially better world. Whether things get better or worse is an open question based on God's sovereignty, the faithfulness or unfaithfulness of the Christian church, and the activity of those hostile or indifferent toward Christian values.

It is likely that "things will get better" in some respects and worse in others; life will improve for some of the world's population and worsen for others. The global picture, and what it means for the church, is the primary focus of our analysis.

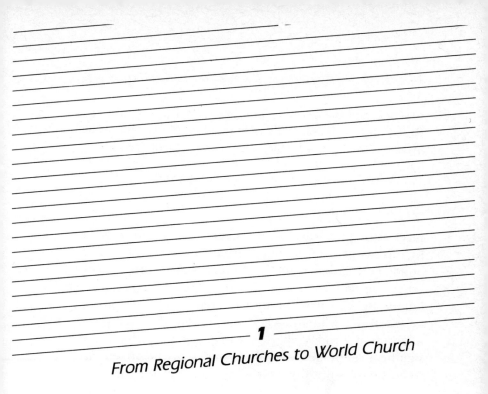

1
From Regional Churches to World Church

Christianity is a global faith. Disciples of Jesus recall His words, "Go into all the world and preach the gospel to every creature" (Mark 16:15). They would be His witnesses "to the ends of the earth" (Acts 1:8). This instruction must have sounded strange—not to say absurd—when first heard in the imperial courts of Rome. Yet, a few centuries later the center of the Empire had become the center of the church. The church increasingly called herself catholic, meaning universal, and for fifteen centuries the city of Rome has been linked more with the Christian church than with civil politics.

A Universal Presence

Today, however, Christianity's claim to universality is true as never before. The handbook *Christianity: A World Faith* states:

15

For centuries Christians have longed and prayed for a genuinely international family of faith. Now at last it has come. During the eighties Christians in the Southern Hemisphere are overtaking northern Christians in numbers. And in many ways Africa, Asia, and Latin America are the centers of vitality and action, more than counterbalancing the decline in Western Europe.[1]

Most major faiths claim universality, but no other religion has created a social organism with the internal bonds and global reach of the Christian church. In this sense the church, for all its fractures and factions, is unique in the earth. Many Christians, however, are unaware of the dramatic ways the church is becoming truly international today. This is a major trend of long-range significance. In fact, we believe this to be the pre-eminent trend today—not only for Christians but for the course of history.

"During the 20th century, Christianity has become the most extensive and universal religion in history," notes David B. Barrett in the *World Christian Encyclopedia* (1982). "There are today Christians and organized Christian churches in every inhabited country on earth. The church is therefore now, for the first time in history, ecumenical in the literal meaning of the word: its boundaries are coextensive with the *oikumene,* 'the whole inhabited world.'"[2]

An average of sixty-five new churches are emerging daily, most in the populous, poorer nations of the Southern Hemisphere, according to Barrett. Some observers say the figure is now twice that.[3]

"The last couple of decades of the twentieth century hold forth more promise for the dynamic spread of the Christian faith around the globe than any other period of time since Jesus turned the water into wine," says missiologist C. Peter Wagner.[4] Though it may be hard to believe, he adds, "at the present time, according to our best calculations, each day welcomes a new increase of at least 78,000 Christians on this planet." The number of Christians compared to world population is now about 30 percent, and the rate of Christian growth seems to be increasing. "Every week approximately one thousand new churches are established in Asia and Africa alone," Wagner claims.[5]

The emergence of Christianity as truly universal in this new, empirical sense, is especially significant when viewed in a world historical perspective. In the nineteen centuries following the life, death, and resurrection of Jesus, Christianity grew to include one-third of all humanity by 1900, but more than 80 percent of these were whites. The *World Christian Encyclopedia* notes that during this period Christianity grew through "a series of 9 massive pulsations or epochs," of which five were times of advance and four were times of retreat. "Already by A.D. 500, 22 percent of mankind were believers in Jesus Christ, but by A.D. 1500 the figure had fallen to only 19 percent."[6] In the optimism surrounding the turn of this century, the wrenching developments to come were not foreseen: "No-one in 1900 expected the massive defections from Christianity that subsequently took place in Western Europe due to secularism, in Russia and later Eastern Europe due to communism, and in the Americas due to materialism."[7]

But in the twentieth century the decline or retrenchment in these traditionally Christian lands has been more than matched by the dramatic growth of the church in the Two-Thirds World (our term for those populous, mostly poorer nations, concentrated in the Southern Hemisphere and sometimes called the Third World). In the "great century" of missions (1815–1914) Christianity grew at a rate of 1.2 percent per decade. Despite great decline in growth in many areas through much of this century, "Christianity has surged ahead in the world's less-developed countries from 83 million in 1900 to 643 million by 1980."[8]

Today Christians number more than half the population in two-thirds of the world's 223 nations and constitute about one-third of all humanity worldwide. About 60 percent of all Christians are urbanized, as compared with a little over 40 percent of the earth's population generally. Most significantly, from being predominantly white, Christianity is now an amalgam of the races and peoples of the world, with whites dropping from more than 80 percent to about 40 percent.[9]

The internationalization of the church, and what this means for tomorrow, is a matter of numbers. But it is much more. Let us look first at world church growth, then at the new age of international missions, and finally at the rise of a new, aggressive generation of Christian leaders and institutions in the Two-Thirds World.

Church Growth in the Two-Thirds World

The church is growing today especially in the Two-Thirds World of Asia, Africa, and Latin America. Church growth has been running ahead of population growth in Latin America for the last few decades. David Barrett notes that "For one hundred years now, the most massive influx into the churches in history has been taking place on the African continent."[10] And the traditional pattern of minimal Christian growth in Asia is changing dramatically with major church growth today in Indonesia, South Korea, the Philippines, and China. (See Chapter 3.)

C. Peter Wagner considers it probable that "the proportion of Christians to the whole population will increase in Asia more than any other region of the world."[11]

Significantly, there is a new Christian harvest among Muslims, according to Peter Wagner. He suggests that "probably more research has been done to develop effective missiological approaches to Muslim evangelism in the past six years than in any other similar period of history."[12] This labor is beginning to bear fruit.

Many factors, including political and economic instability, have provided fertile soil for the growth of Christianity. Since 1942 nearly one hundred new nations have come into being as colonialism crumbled and countries won independence. In just fifteen years, from 1945 to 1960, forty new nations totalling 800 million people (more than one-fourth of the population at that time) were born.[13]

Yet the advance of the church is often due to the vision and commitment of local Christian leaders, regardless of political and economic conditions. Consider the following examples from widely separated places on the globe.

In 1979 Chris Marantika, an Indonesian, founded the interdenominational Evangelical Theological Seminary of Indonesia on the island of Java. His goal: to start 1,000 churches by the year 2000; a church in every Indonesian village by the year 2015. (Fifty thousand Indonesian villages are without a church!) After one year his students and staff had planted 27 churches. (A requirement for graduation is to plant at least one church.) By the end of the 1985 school year 294 students had graduated after establishing 327 new congregations in cooperation with the parent denominations of the students.

Since students were in class four days a week, they could plant churches only within 100 miles of campus.

This meant more seminaries were needed. Marantika has already begun four branch campuses and plans to have fourteen campuses in operation by 1990, adding satellite campuses each year until the total reaches 450 by 2015.

One secret to Marantika's success is his rejection of church-planting principles of self-support, self-propagation, and self-government which he was taught while attending North American seminaries. After much intellectual struggle he concluded that "self, self, and self is not biblical."

"People were telling me that ideal missionary work is doing something that can be supported completely from within the country," he said. "But my dream is Indonesia for Christ. We can't do it if we have to do it by ourselves." His alternative approach is to pray together, pay together, and proclaim together. The support and cooperation of churches, mission agencies, and church leaders from many parts of the world are essential.[14]

In Colombia strong Protestant church growth began among peasants in the late fifties, spread to the cities in the seventies, and today urban churches are flourishing. Colombia "is moving closer and closer to anarchy," said Eugene Wittig, executive vice-president of OMS International. "Yet as a result, we are seeing more openness to the gospel than ever before, especially in the middle and upper classes."[15] While the Protestant church represents only 2 to 4 percent of the population, the Roman Catholic Church which claims 95 percent of Colombians, "is beginning to experience spiritual renewal through a growing charismatic movement."[16] David Howard, general secretary of the World Evangelical Fellowship, says significant church growth began after the Second Vatican Council (1962–65). "When Pope John XXIII told people they should start reading the Bible, it was like the floodgates were opened," Howard reports. "From that time on, there was great church growth."[17]

Not all significant growth is in the Two-Thirds World. Consider this report from the Soviet Union: Vladimir Veriga recently moved from a small town near Moscow to serve the Russian Orthodox Cathedral of St. Nicholas in San Francisco. He reports a renewal of religious belief and practice in the Soviet Union. "There are fifty million practicing Orthodox," said Veriga, "seventeen hundred churches, about fifty thousand priests, four seminaries and two academies." He says church membership is growing, even among government officials and young people.

Another new development is that for the first time in all the history of the church, women have been accepted into theological studies at the Leningrad Theological School. Though women are not allowed to become priests in the Russian Orthodox church, many are obtaining master's degrees in theology to teach or serve in other ways. A decade ago the Moscow Theological Seminary had 180 applicants and accepted 60. In 1985 the school had 380 applicants and accepted 120 new students for the priesthood.[18]

During a visit to San Francisco Bishop Clement, vicar of the Patriarch of Moscow, said that practicing believers are found in many high government positions. Despite Communist Party atheism, many agencies of government "include believers as well as nonbelievers." Clement also noted that while the Russian Orthodox church is by far the largest denomination in Russia, "there are Georgian Orthodox, All-Believers Orthodox, Catholic, Baptist, Lutheran, and also Buddhists and Jews."[19]

The dramatic story of missions in the twentieth century includes the growth of mission agencies working with unreached peoples and the planting of new churches where growth had previously been negligible. Two such organizations are Wycliffe Bible Translators and Youth With A Mission. According to Waldron Scott, Wycliffe Bible Translators, which was founded in 1934, has become "the largest Protestant missionary society in the world," with more than 2,500 missionaries working among 700 "people groups" around the world.[20] Meanwhile Youth With A Mission, only 25 years old, has deployed thousands of youthful missionaries from many nations and established more than 100 training bases. According to World Vision, YWAM today has more missionaries in active service than any other agency.

Also important is the emergence of new Christian institutions in the Two-Thirds World. We take North American institutions for granted, but parallel institutions in education, publishing, and communications are being developed in many of the newer churches of mission origin. One can only imagine the impact worldwide as these structures emerge in force.

Internationalizing World Missions

Particularly important is the rise of mission agencies in lands which we in North America have traditionally thought of as "the mission field." In the nineteenth century North America, especially, was the great sending base for missions. Now we are seeing an increase in mission agencies among churches which for decades received missionaries from North America and Europe. The receiving countries are becoming the sending countries.

For example, Brazil now has more than 40 organizations that send missionaries to other parts of the world.

By 1972 approximately 200 Christian missions from the Two-Thirds World had deployed about 3,400 missionaries throughout the world. By 1980 the total had risen to 368 agencies sending 13,000 missionaries. Wagner calculates, "If that rate of increase continues, the third-world Protestant missionary force may project to over 50,000 by the end of the century."[21]

These indigenous agencies reflect the missionary impulse of the newer churches of mission origin and the rise of leadership within these churches. Their efforts are directed both to evangelism cross-culturally within their own nations as well as to foreign missions. Waldron Scott notes that "such endeavors have mushroomed in recent years. Now numbering more than 32,500, Third-World missionaries are expanding their areas of service rapidly."[22]

Of course, not all former "mission churches" see themselves as missionary churches. One U.S. churchman, after spending six months in Korea, reports that many Christians there "do not yet see their mission role and are preoccupied with building new churches." Bishop Gerald Bates of the Free Methodist Church adds, "I see Third-World missions as important but overdramatized," tending "to obscure the distinctives of definition of what is missions in order to emphasize the extent of the movement." And missiologist William Cook suggests that "Third World agencies tend to be unduly dominated by U.S. mission structures."

The missionary outreach of North America is, in fact, continuing to grow. North American Protestant missionaries overseas numbered 34,460 in 1969 and 53,494 in 1979, an increase of more than 50 percent over the course of the decade.[23] Missiologist C. Peter Wagner suggests:

The momentum begun in the seventies seems to be increasing in the eighties. The number of agencies and societies committed to sending out missionaries will undoubtedly increase through the end of the century. . . . Mission societies will continue to start in the U.S.A. and other Western nations, but in all probability a much greater number proportionately will be formed in the third world.[24]

Another recent development in missions, perhaps related to the so-called entrepreneurial explosion, is the rise of short-term missionary service. About one-third of the current North American missionary force of over 53,000 are short-term missionaries, and at any one time about 8,500 short-term missionaries are on the field.[25]

"We are in the springtime of Christian missions," concludes Wagner.[26]

Shift in the Church's Center of Gravity

These and related developments are producing a revolution in the church of historically long-range import: a shift of the church's center of gravity from the North and West (mainly Europe and North America) to the Two-Thirds World—the populous, poorer nations located predominately in the Southern Hemisphere. *Christianity: A World Faith* notes: "At the beginning of the twentieth century, Christianity was a faith mainly of the Northern Hemisphere. This is no longer true. During the eighties Christians in the South will become more numerous than those in the North."[27]

In 1900 the Northern Hemisphere (Europe, North America, and the USSR) counted 462 million Christians, 83 percent of the world total, while south of the equator there were approximately 96 million Christians, or 17 percent of the total. By 1980 the church in the Southern

Hemisphere had grown to 700 million, nearly half of the world total of over 1.4 billion.

In these eighty years Africa's percentage of the world church went from less than 2 percent to 14 percent, while the European church went from 50 percent to under 30 percent of the world total.[28] *The church of the historically Christian nations of the North is becoming the minority church in the world.*

In light of these global developments, John Naisbitt's megatrend of the population shift from North to South has some significance. Let us look at this U.S. trend in light of the broader picture of the global church.

Naisbitt is speaking primarily of migration within the United States—a shift in population to the West, Southwest, and Florida. For a variety of reasons, people and industries are increasing rapidly in the new South particularly as the "sunset industries" of the Frost Belt decline and the new electronics, biogenic, human services, and related industries grow in the Sun Belt.

Interestingly, Naisbitt says virtually nothing about the new immigration which has brought millions of Hispanics (especially Mexicans), Asians, and others to the United States in the past decade and a half. Hispano-Americans will soon outnumber Afro-Americans, and we expect the high level of immigration from Asia to continue as well.[29] From the standpoint of the church and of global realities, this is probably a much more significant trend. And the influx of Hispanics relates to the broader trends we are noting in this chapter.

The north to south shift in the U.S. does, however, have at least three implications for Christians:

1. *This shift provides considerable opportunity and responsibility for evangelism, church planting, and prophetic ministries in the U.S. South and Southwest.* First, there is the obvious matter of numbers—millions of people needing to hear and respond to the gospel, or to have a nominal Christian faith turned into a vital one. In addition, students of church growth tell us that people recently uprooted are more open to changes and new commitments. Extensive church planting and other ministries must be carried out in these areas of burgeoning population. The new societies emerging in these areas must be Christianized as thoroughly as possible. Here are opportunities for significant and redemptive ministry.

2. *The church also bears a great responsibility to those areas and people "left behind," and particularly to the urban poor of the Frost Belt, also called the Rust Belt.* Just as the more affluent and economically mobile population moves to the suburbs, leaving a growing concentration of the urban poor, so the broader move from North to South leaves many urban communities increasingly impoverished. Eroding tax bases, both personal and corporate, further weaken the network of social services for such communities.

The church is always commissioned to carry the gospel to the poor, and to be an advocate for the poor and marginalized. The church will not be biblically faithful if it simply follows the secular trend from North to South; from decaying areas to developing areas.

3. *The shift from North to South is part of a broader picture of demographic and economic changes in North America.* Naisbitt notes that this trend is linked to the move from a national to a world economy,[30] with the key states of Florida, California, and Texas becoming increasingly international in outlook and interdependence. Naisbitt quotes former California Senator S. I. Hayakawa: "What happens in the Philippines, Japan, and Korea has a greater impact on us and is of more immediate interest to us than most events in Massachusetts."[31]

We are in a world of expanding global interdependence. The internationalizing of the church parallels broader developments throughout the world. As a result, the church will increasingly interact with a world which is consciously global and international.

New Age of World Christianity

The church and the self-perception of every genuine Christian believer will be different as we move into the twenty-first century. While provincialism certainly will continue, increasingly, Christians will understand the church as a reality transcending any one culture, language, or ethnic tradition.

It would be naive, however, to suppose that the church will move smoothly into this new phase. Traditions and national loyalties are strong and often undermine a wholesome expression of the gospel. Thus some of these internationalizing trends will themselves produce tensions and struggles.

David Lowes Watson of the United Methodist Board of Discipleship says that the internationalizing of the world missionary enterprise "is a time bomb for the North American church, which is still fighting its dated battle over the Enlightenment, and has the power (and bad manners) to inflict it on the rest of the world." An evangelical denominational leader in the U.S. comments that the "largest struggle will be for the so-called sending church to accept the role of a receiving church" as the newer churches mature and develop their own leadership.

Nevertheless, we may expect to see a world church emerging which bears the following characteristics:

- A church of growing ethnic and cultural diversity, increasingly approximating the biblical picture of "a great multitude . . . of all nations, tribes, peoples, and tongues" (Rev. 7:9).
- A church of growing mutual respect for the leadership, styles, ministries, and traditions of other Christian believers. Perhaps the Pauline picture of one body made up of many interdependent parts and gifts (see 1 Cor. 12) will take on a new global meaning.
- An increasingly urban church. Though much of the church will remain rural, especially in China, the major Christian centers will be the "world class cities" of the globe. These will contain the greatest concentrations of Christians and be the centers of the most significant Christian institutions.
- A servant church where ministry to the poor, oppressed, and suffering is both a high priority and a practical program. We expect that if the new world church is truly international, interdependent, and biblically faithful, it will also be a suffering church.

With these trends and tendencies, the opportunity for a dynamic world church is present.

An alternative scenario pictures increasingly isolationist and nationalistic churches, serving secular, political, and economic forces more than God's kingdom. This has happened too often in history. Emerging trends suggest cautious optimism, however, for a new age of world Christianity dominated more by the spirit of Jesus than by secular or satanic forces.

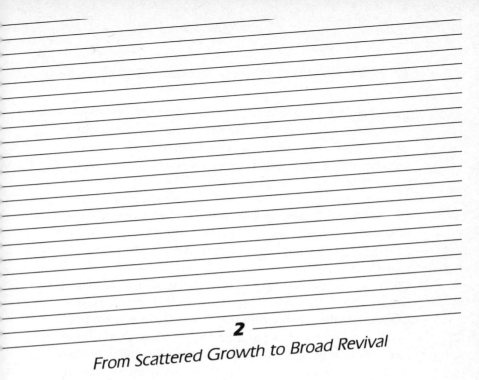

2
From Scattered Growth to Broad Revival

Worldwide revival is the expectation of a growing number of Christians. New hope stems in part from what is already happening in places like South Korea and Central Africa where the church has experienced tremendous spiritual and numerical growth. Such news sparks hope that something similar may occur in North America.

Based on his organization's surveys, George Gallup, Jr., suggested a few years back that "the final two decades of the twentieth century could be a period of profound religious renewal in our society . . . . People in all walks of life are hungry for depth and meaning in their lives and want to gain a new understanding of their relationship to God."[1]

As evidence, Gallup points to a dramatic increase in religious education programs, Bible studies, and programs of evangelization. He notes, "The real news of what is going on in the religious life of Americans today is *outside* formal worship. The proportion of adult Americans who say they have received religious education or training other than during their worship service within the last two years has grown from 17 percent in 1978 to 26 percent in our latest survey." Gallup's survey reported that Bible study among teens has moved from 27 to 41 percent, and adults who have tried to encourage someone to believe in Jesus Christ increased from 44 to 53 percent.[2]

These findings suggest that a 200-year-old trend continues. In 1776 only 7 percent of U.S. citizens were church members. This figure rose to 20 percent by 1850, to 36 percent by 1900, and in 1976 approached 60 percent.[3] To put these figures into perspective, consider Peter Wagner's observation that "more Americans attend church in an average week than attend all professional baseball, basketball, and football games combined in an average year!"[4]

Ralph Winter of the U.S. Center for World Mission contends that Christians in North America are unrealistically pessimistic about church growth in their own culture. In 1975 he noted that while we may be moving into a post-western era, there is no evidence that the world is moving into a post-Christian era. In fact, the number of Christians in the nonwestern world increased 140 percent from 1950 to 1975 while the general population grew only 42 percent. Winter concludes, "by 1975 Christianity . . . was continuing to outgrow all other religious movements in global size and influence."[5]

It may help to set the current scene in perspective. Noting the dramatic progress of the outreach arm of the North American church (particularly by evangelicals), in the last forty years, Joseph Bayly writes:

We inherited one national youth movement—Christian Endeavor, working through the local church—and a Sunday evening young people's meeting, often attended by adults. We bequeath a sophisticated understanding of teens and young adults applied within the local church and outside the church by thousands of professionals. Parachurch youth organizations we founded include Youth for Christ, Young Life, Inter-Varsity Christian Fellowship, and Campus Crusade for Christ.

We inherited scattered local radio programs, while the rest of religious radio—except for Charles E. Fuller's "Old Fashioned Revival Hour"—was monopolized by the National Council of Churches. We bequeath an end to the monopoly (and the National Council's power), innumerable local radio and television programs, several networks, many independent stations, and an electronic church that takes in $500 million dollars a year.

We inherited a few publishers and several hundred bookstores. We bequeath a hundred publishers and five thousand bookstores.[6]

Whether such "success" equals genuine spiritual renewal is, of course, a major question. The church may simply be getting fatter, not healthier. Nevertheless, many people anticipate a deep and genuine movement of renewal. Dr. William Abraham, professor of evangelism at Perkins School of Theology in Dallas, Texas, foresees a "coming great revival" that is broad-based, due partly to the influence of charismatic renewal. He writes:

Among a host of groups within and without the mainline churches, there is an urge for renewal that shows no indication of abating. The charismatic movement, despite its faults, has broken down the old denominational barriers, . . . has retrieved vital elements of the original gospel message, has vastly extended the ministry of the people of God, and has brought fresh vigor and life to a multitude of defeated Christians. A new generation of young converts has emerged, keen to look critically at the recent past without abandoning the central tenets of the Christian gospel. Thus there is a vast army of new Christians hungry for initiation into a modern version of the Christian faith that will integrate deep piety, social action, and classical theology in a penetrating expression of the Christian gospel.[7]

Pentecostal/Charismatic Growth

Pentecostalism and the charismatic movement together constitute the first major Christian renewal in history to have roots in North America. Dr. Russell Spittler of Fuller Theological Seminary traces the dimensions of the Pentecostal/charismatic explosion of this century:

> Today, Pentecostal believers in over 1,200 of their own denominations number, worldwide, in excess of 51 million. When the newer Charismatics are added . . . the total exceeds 100 million . . . . With no more than a handful of identifiable adherents at the opening of the twentieth century, Pentecostal Christians within three generations have become the largest sector of Protestantism. And in the mid-1980s, close to 10 percent of the world's Roman Catholics can be identified as Catholic Pentecostals.[8]

Charismatic renewal has become pervasive in most major Protestant denominations, as well as in Roman Catholicism. The renewal cuts across economic, ethnic, and educational boundaries to include Christian fellowship groups on college campuses, the television ministries of Oral Roberts, Pat Robertson, and others, small local Bible study groups loosely affiliated with denominational bodies, and the influence of the Full Gospel Business Men's Fellowship International.

Charles Hummel writes that charismatic renewal is unique:

> It cannot be traced to one outstanding leader and his followers with the stamp of their doctrinal and organizational convictions. . . . The charismatic renewal started as a pattern of events in the lives of a wide variety of Christians. This pattern comes to focus in the exercise of the full range of spiritual gifts (charisms) for strengthening the body of Christ in worship, evangelism, and service.[9]

The Second Vatican Council of the early sixties helped prepare the way for charismatic renewal in the Roman Catholic Church, as did the Cursillo movement and Protestant neo-Pentecostalism. Since the sixties, widespread charismatic renewal has swept through South Korea, Central Africa, Latin America, and some South American countries such as Brazil and Chile, as well as North America. Author Vinson Synan argues that charismatic renewal "constitutes the most vital and fastest-growing movement in the church since the days of the Reformation."[10]

Expectation of a Third Wave

Some look for a major Christian renewal worldwide, especially among charismatic Christians, in a "third wave" of revival. Synan summarizes this hope as follows:

> Today . . . millions of people . . . believe that the church is now in the "latter-rain" stage of God's dealing with mankind. They believe that the greatest miracles and victories in the history of the church will come just before the appearing of the Lord. They fervently believe that all the gifts of the Spirit have been restored to the church and that the bride of Christ will be caught up in a shout of victory rather than in a moan of defeat.[11]

Synan believes that the expectation of major revival will grow.

By 1983 some leaders were talking about a "third wave" of Pentecostalism which would enter the mainline churches with little struggle or notoriety. This "third wave" would be a successor to the first two, i.e. the classical Pentecostals and the charismatics. The new wave would be made up of evangelicals in the major traditional churches who would receive and exercise the gifts of the Spirit without accepting the labels.[12]

In a similar vein Peter Wagner has written, "I see in the eighties an opening of the straightline evangelicals and other Christians to the supernatural work of the Holy Spirit that the Pentecostals and charismatics have experienced, but without becoming either charismatic or Pentecostal."[13]

Part of the picture here is the recent growth of the "signs and wonders" emphasis associated especially with John Wimber and Vineyard Ministries. Peter Wagner considers that "power evangelism—accompanied by signs and wonders" will be a trend of great significance in coming decades, and *World Christian* publisher Gordon Aeschliman says, "It is my guess that history books will show 'signs and wonders' churches to be the fastest-growing [sector of the] church from 1980–1995," though he adds that "desire for renewal is strong across most denominations."

Evangelist Leighton Ford cautions, however, that the anticipation of revival will have a "very mixed effect, especially if *power* overpowers *holiness*." Similarly, missiologist William Cook warns that while genuine revival is to be desired, yet "revivalism and chiliasm in Latin America are providing a convenient escape from social awareness and involvement."

It is true, as sociologist David Moberg observes, that "Every century seems an 'end-time' to many who live in it." David Lowes Watson says, "Apocalyptic is a mere fad; but interest in the eschatological cutting edge of the gospel is highly significant" for the future of the church. On the other hand, poet Luci Shaw suggests that despite expectation of revival today, there is "not nearly enough concerted prayer and heart-concern through which the Holy Spirit may work."

However one may evaluate *theologically* the claims and hopes for a major revival, *sociologically* the hope is significant, especially if it raises expectations of what God can do in the present time. History shows that major renewal movements of the past, such as the evangelical revivals in Europe and England in the eighteenth century, were spurred in part by expectations that fed on accounts of what was happening elsewhere. For example, news of the Great Awakening in New England nurtured revival expectations in Great Britain. Something parallel to this may be happening today on a global scale. Specifically, renewal and church growth in the Two-Thirds World appears to be having a reflexive impact in North America and elsewhere.

Evangelicals' Turning to Liturgical Worship

A different trend is the growing interest among evangelicals in historic liturgical worship patterns—what Wheaton College theologian Robert Webber calls "Evangelicals on the Canterbury Trail." Webber writes, "I am overwhelmed by the number of people I meet who are either journeying" toward liturgical worship or are "at least somewhat influenced by the concern to restore aspects of historical Christianity inadequately represented in their own church."[14]

Though we know of no statistics, and though this is largely a North American development, we have encountered it frequently enough to indicate that a movement is underway. It goes beyond evangelical attraction to liturgical churches to include the increasing centrality of the Eucharist in many nonliturgical churches and Christian communities. It includes also the attraction many evangelicals feel toward the Orthodox tradition, most evident in the founding of the Evangelical Orthodox Church by a group of Christians from typically evangelical backgrounds.

Some of us know people from our own denominational traditions who have found a spiritual home in the Episcopal Church. Robert Webber describes what apparently is the common experience of many:

> For me, Anglicanism preserves in its worship and sacraments the sense of mystery that rationalistic Christianity of either the liberal or evangelical sort seems to deny. I found myself longing for an experience of worship that went beyond either emotionalism or intellectualism. I believe I've found that for myself in the Anglican tradition. I also felt a need for visible and tangible symbols that I could touch, feel, and experience with my senses. This need is met in the reality of Christ presented to me through the sacraments."[15]

Webber says he has been attracted to the Anglican tradition for six reasons: "Mystery, worship, sacraments, historical identity, ecumenical affirmation, and holistic spirituality."[16]

Somewhat related is the much-publicized case of Thomas Howard, a prominent evangelical scholar who recently embraced Roman Catholicism and who writes:

Enough people are following a similar route [to more traditional liturgical worship] to warrant our using the term "a movement in the church.". . . Something is causing thousands of stoutly loyal evangelical men and women to inquire into matters of the gravest antiquity and gravity [and seek an evangelicalism] rooted once again in the mystery and authority of the Church understood as one, holy, catholic, and apostolic.[17]

What is the significance of this move toward historic liturgical worship? First, the movement signals a genuine spiritual hunger and quest on the part of many orthodox believers for a deeper and more meaningful faith. It would be a misreading to see it as a drift from spiritual depth. Rather, it is one form of renewal for many Christians. Second, in its stress on the historic means of grace, particularly the Eucharist, this movement holds some promise for deepening the spiritual life and dynamism of the church. Historically and in the early church, the Lord's Supper was much more central to the church's life than has been true for much of Protestantism. A renewed stress on the Eucharist—not as empty ritual, but as a vital means of growth—may well prove to be a factor leading to a "coming great revival" in the church.

Renewal in Mainline Denominations

For nearly a century many mainline denominations drifted away from traditional Christian orthodoxy. Now renewal currents in major denominations may signal a reversal of this trend.

Sources of this renewal include the charismatic movement, the Good News movement in the United Methodist Church, and similar groups in other mainline denominations, as well as growing intellectual and spiritual disillusionment with traditional liberalism. Do these developments indicate a trend toward a more biblical gospel, or the likelihood of more schisms and controversy?

David L. McKenna, president of Asbury Theological Seminary, predicts: "Sooner or later the leadership of mainline denominations will have to become more responsive to the spiritual needs and moral issues which rise first as cries of help and later as warning lights from the people in the pew." He predicts: "Evangelical pastors will remain loyal to the denomination but withdraw from the politics of the hierarchy in order to build the local church as the last hope for renewal. The greatest loss will be the younger generation of individuals and families who . . . place a higher value upon spiritual nurture and social compatability than upon theological distinctions and denominational loyalty. Simply put, they would rather switch than fight."

McKenna sees, however, several encouraging signs. He cites the observations of Bishop Emerson Colaw of the United Methodist Church who, despite declining denominational membership, sees dramatic growth in adult Bible studies. McKenna notes that in these groups "members open themselves to the authority of the Word and experience the transcendent. The bishop is quick to define this turnabout as evidence of evangelical spirit and mainline strength coming together."

Lyle Schaller says, "In every generation, a church must take out a new franchise." This means asking three questions: Who is around? What are their needs? How are we speaking to their needs? "If the mainline church is to 'take out a new franchise' for the future," McKenna suggests, "these questions must be asked and the answer that comes from the laity at the grassroots must be heard. Then, if we liken mainline churches to General Motors in the auto industry, we can say, 'What's good for mainline denominations is good for the church as a whole.'"[18]

Charismatic renewal has been a major factor in the resurgence of mainline church bodies. This renewal now includes Methodist, Lutheran, Roman Catholic, Episcopal, and Presbyterian groups. Explaining the growing acceptance of Pentecostalism and charismatic renewal, United Methodist theologian Theodore Runyon suggests:

> If outward authorities cannot speak with convincing certainty, inevitably we turn . . . inward, and search for certainty there. We yearn for some personal experience that—to use Abraham Maslow's term—can serve as a "peak experience," a moment of undeniable reality, a lodestar around which the other things in life can be located, sorted out, and held together in a meaningful whole.[19]

Charismatic renewal has been the vehicle for a fresh (and often first-time) encounter with God for many in mainline churches.

Frankly, competition may be another factor spurring renewal in mainline churches. *Time* magazine has commented that fundamentalist and evangelical groups "offer a clearly defined presentation of Christianity that is persuasive to an increasing number of [North] Americans. The prosperity of these churches is striking at a time when mainline Protestant groups are eroding." The article further notes that while major denominations have declined by 4.6 million since 1965, in the same period Southern Baptists alone increased by 3.4 million.[20]

Major denominations have suffered from low birthrate among members, the population shift to Sunbelt states, and the difficulty liberal churches experience in holding the allegiance of teens and young adults. Southern Baptist pastor W. A. Criswell of Dallas, Texas, thinks liberal theology is the culprit: "Wherever liberalism places its leprous hand, there is death."[21] Other complex and diverse factors are involved, however. These include the typical negative effects of institutional aging, theological shifts in seminary faculties, and in some cases population shifts from central cities to the suburbs.

For many, conservative churches are attractive because they provide definite answers to religious questions. They offer moral guidance, the prospect of a life that is meaningful and wholesome, and spiritual redemption through a personal relationship with Jesus Christ. Mainline churches which are experiencing renewal likewise are learning to meet the human need for direct relationship with God. In this connection George Gallup comments:

> I believe religious leaders and educators can be hopeful about the future. The new spiritual quest we are noting today could indeed develop [into] religious renewal. If the churches of [North] America are able to satisfy the spiritual hunger of the population and awaken people to the realization that they are important in God's eyes, the final two decades of this century could be a period of unusual vigor, health, and vitality for the churches of this nation and for the spiritual and overall health of society.[22]

As evidence, Gallup cites survey results showing that high percentages of those who say religion is not very important in their lives wish their own beliefs were stronger, want religion to play a greater role in people's lives in society as a whole, and desire religious training for their children.[23]

Resurgence within the Roman Catholic Church

Some observers see a significant resurgence of Roman Catholicism beyond the impact of the Catholic charismatic renewal. If so, this must rank as a major trend, for the Roman Catholic church is the largest body in Christendom.

According to Thomas Stransky, one of the "long-term effects" of the Second Vatican Council has been the upgraded role of the laity in the life and self-understanding of the church. "The laity are appreciating that they are the essence of the church, not its second-class citizens. As people of God, lay Christians are responsible for their own faith, for the good of the institutional church, and for the evangelization of the world."[24] To the degree this is true, it is a sign of fundamental renewal.

One grassroots example of greater lay leadership comes from Flint, Michigan, where, due to a critical shortage of priests, Ken Berger and his wife, Pat, have assumed the financial and spiritual leadership of Sacred Heart Catholic Church.[25] Similarly, at St. Ignatius of Loyola Church in Urbana, Maryland, layman John Manley is responsible for the church and its 320 families. Manley, married and the father of three teen-agers, is a juvenile services administrator who was ordained as a deacon in the Roman Catholic archdiocese in Baltimore in 1976.

The Berger and Manley families are not pioneers. The trend began in 1971 when the first six married deacons in the U.S. were ordained in Baltimore. By 1986 their numbers had risen to 7,204 nationwide. A deacon is allowed to administer every service except the mass, and he cannot hear confessions. Manley notes that this innovation was common practice in the early days of the church, when bishops traveled from parish to parish to administer services and say mass.[26]

Rev. Arthur Bastress, coordinator of the diaconate for the Baltimore archdiocese, says the permanent diaconate "is the route bishops are going to utilize" as the shortage of priests becomes acute. Church records indicate that while the number of priests dropped by 1,600 between 1976 and 1986, the Catholic church has grown by 3.6 million members.[27]

In a similar vein, Gallup and Poling note in *The Search for America's Faith* a "new flowering of the faith and a new confidence about being a Catholic Christian in America." On the basis of their research, they project "a golden era of growth and power ahead" for U.S. Catholics. They note that Catholics increased from 25 to 28 percent of the nation's population between 1970 and 1980 (largely through Hispanic immigration), and that Catholic church attendance has begun to rise.[28] Additionally, in U.S. urban areas the decline of public education may well spark a rejuvenation of the extensive Catholic parochial school system.

New Dialogue between Catholics, Protestants, and Orthodox

One surprise of the last decade in North America has been the opening of dialogue, fellowship, and some joint action between evangelical Protestants and Roman Catholics, both charismatic and noncharismatic. In place of "a Berlin Wall between evangelical Christians and Roman Catholics," says Joseph Bayly, is coming a new "spirit of love and rapprochement on the basis of the Bible rather than fear and hatred."[29] Examples include:

- The American Society of Missiology and its quarterly review, *Missiology,* which regularly features articles by both Catholics and Protestants;

- A series of ecumenical renewal conferences sponsored by the Word of God community in Ann Arbor, Michigan (itself a mix of Catholics and Protestants in one charismatic community), which have included Orthodox as well as Protestant and Catholic participants;
- Increasing numbers of neighborhood Bible study groups in which both Catholics and Protestants gather;
- Joint Catholic-Protestant publishing efforts, and the publication by Catholic houses such as Orbis and Paulist of major works by evangelical authors Charles Kraft, Orlando Costas, William Cook, and others.

Another example of dialogue and cooperation took place in 1985 when public letters between Pope John Paul II and Presiding Bishop James Crumley of the Lutheran Church in America pledged to build closer relations. The letters may be the first time the pope and the head of a Protestant church body have formally exchanged such direct comments on relations between their churches. "We have been heartened by the growing understanding of our common faith and we have been encouraged at the theological convergence that is developing between Lutherans and Roman Catholics," Crumley said in his letter.

John Paul said the official theological dialogues and subsequent contact between Lutherans and Catholics have "made us increasingly aware of how close we are to each other in the 'heart of the gospel' . . . . We still experience anguish because full unity has not yet been achieved." Divisions among Christians, he said, "obscure the face of Christ, making it more difficult for the world to believe."[30]

The letters reflect a growing theological consensus that began in 1963 when official Lutheran-Catholic talks were initiated. In the twenty-two years of officially sanctioned dialogue, theologians from the two church bodies have reached "substantial convergence" on such key doctrinal issues as baptism, the nature of the Eucharist (Holy Communion), ministry, and justification (how a person is saved).[31] The continuing dialogue between Roman Catholicism and the Anglican communion, begun in 1966, also reportedly is beginning to bear fruit.[32]

Within Protestantism, evangelicals have been showing increased openness to dialogue and interdenominational cooperation. Incorporating Baptists, Holiness and Pentecostal groups, the Anabaptist tradition, and Reformational-Confessional bodies, evangelicalism from the start has transcended denominational barriers. Today the scope of the "evangelical" designation includes many Roman Catholics, Anglicans and Episcopalians, and other Christians who are basically evangelical in their understanding and practice of the faith, whether or not they are Protestant.

Speaking of Protestant evangelicalism since World War II, James Hunter writes, "Christianity, even in the most intransigent quarters, has become 'civil.'"[33] Moderation and mutual acceptance will probably continue to grow on into the twenty-first century, though many fundamentalists see this as a weakness in the evangelical movement and condemn it as watered-down Christianity (though some sectors of fundamentalism have muted their tone). Evangelicals counter that cooperation and openness among Christians produce more effective outreach. In the evangelical view, conservative theology and open-minded cooperation are not incompatible.

We have witnessed many examples of effective evangelical cooperation. Billy Graham crusades depend heavily on local congregations working together across confessional lines to evangelize the community. World Relief Corporation, Evangelicals for Social Action, and Bread for the World (covering a rather broad theological spectrum) are other important examples.

This greater openness and cooperation among evangelical Christians does not seem to signal a more liberal theological shift. It appears that, despite fundamentalist fears, cooperation does not inexorably lead to liberalism. Demographic data suggest that Protestants rank high in opposition to abortion (95.3 percent), extramarital sexual intercourse (96.7 percent), homosexuality (88.7 percent) and opposition to divorce (66.7 percent).[34]

Worldwide Renewal

Christians frequently hear of past revivals, awakenings, and renewal movements, yet these events seem disconnected from modern reality. Our understanding of them is often stereotyped, or even mythical. But every age is potentially an age of renewal. Key figures in past renewals often were weak or lopsided characters like ourselves.

Significantly, renewal and revival are happening in many scattered places around the globe, sparking a growing expectation for revival. For the first time in history, the world has become one interconnected communications network. Increasingly, what Christians do is "not done in a corner" (Acts 26:26). The world may be poised as never before to hear and respond to the Good News.

We are seeing unprecedented Christian growth worldwide, evidence of new spiritual hunger in the traditionally Christian lands of North America and Europe, evangelical and charismatic renewal in major denominations, new cooperation across denominational lines, and a quest for deeper experience of worship and spirituality among many evangelical Protestants. Together these currents suggest the rebirth of the Christian faith in North America and worldwide. They give more hope for a revival of broader scope than anything in history.

Renewals such as what historian Bernard Semmel called "the Methodist Revolution" in England in the eighteenth century have shaped the course of history more than most people today realize.[35] And we cannot understand the history of the United States without reference to the social and political impact of religious revival over two centuries.

What will happen now that the world is becoming a global city just at the time when in many places the Christian church is finding new life? Christian revival may be the wave of the future.

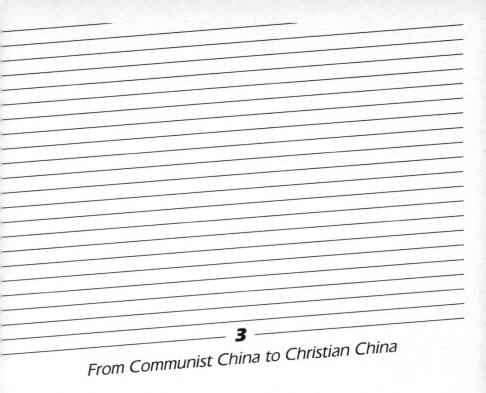

3

From Communist China to Christian China

After a visit to China, *New York Times* correspondent Fox Butterfield reported:

> I was not prepared for an energetic, candid, middle-aged Party member who was chairman of her local street committee, the lowest level of government organization. One evening when I stopped by her fifth-floor walkup apartment, I found she was reading the Bible. I was incredulous. She explained that recently a forty-five-year old man had knocked on her door, claiming to be a friend of a woman she knew. He wondered if she believed in God or had read the Bible.
>
> In the end, my friend accepted his offering of a Chinese-language Bible. She was reading it with evident interest. "You don't know it," she advised me, "but Christianity is spreading rapidly in China because people are so disillusioned with communism." If she had been a political dissident, I would have been doubtful. But she was the neighborhood Party boss.[1]

Another observer, G. Thompson Brown (who was born in China), reports:

> There is no doubt that Christianity has gained a receptive ear in post-Mao China. The evidence for this is overwhelming: the crowded churches on Sunday, the house congregation phenomenon, the thirst for the Scriptures, the number of young men and women seeking to enter the seminary. People have become believers from all walks of life—including those who are members of the Communist party.[2]

Rebirth of a Church

"China is a nation in transition," says Dr. James Hudson Taylor, great-grandson of pioneer China missionary Hudson Taylor. Now director of the Overseas Missionary Fellowship (formerly China Inland Mission), Taylor is one of the most knowledgeable observers of developments in China over the past half-century.

These and many other observers document a trend of significance to the whole world: the rebirth of the Christian church in China. Before examining what we can learn from this trend, let us see what caused this surprising development.

China is undergoing basic changes socially, economically, and politically. Taylor notes, "The agricultural segment of society has been released from the terror of the commune, and the family unit has been re-established as the basic unit of production in agriculture." This is especially significant in a nation which is still 80 percent rural.

Perhaps even more important is the spiritual vacuum accompanying these changes. "Young people are disillusioned with their leaders and with the ideology of the nation," says Taylor. A letter printed in the Chinese

Communist journal, *China Youth*, forcefully makes the point: "I was born into a Communist family but I am totally disillusioned and feel like committing suicide—I don't see any future in life. All I want to do is live for myself: that's what I see everybody else doing."[3]

The resurgence of the church in China is tied to historic Chinese culture and to new political and economic developments of the past decade. Jay and Linda Adams, journalists who spent four years in China, report that the Chinese "resent—some actively, the majority almost unconsciously—the oppression and inconvenience of their form of government but prefer to finesse it rather than challenge it outright." "China is a small town of one billion people," they suggest; "the whole country operates underground much of the time."

The new (or newly-discovered) vitality of the Chinese church needs to be seen against a broader cultural background.

Being Chinese in the 1980s is less a commitment to Mao, Marx, and the motherland than it is a commitment to one another—billions of small relationships becoming one great whole. Foreigners will continue to misread the Chinese and their future role in the world unless they appreciate this point.[4]

A key word is *quanxi,* roughly meaning "relationships" or "connections," based on face-to-face interaction and personal influence.

The Chinese obsession with human feelings, their ties to family and neighborhood, their commitment to the simple idea of being Chinese, somehow bind together the world's most populous nation. . . . The relationships of trust that have survived the cultural revolution are now all the more precious and important because of that experience.[5]

"The cultural revolution was a turning point in the life of every Chinese adult alive today", note the Adams.[6] It may also have been a turning point for the church. It effectively destroyed the faith of many in the new Communist order, thus at the same time bringing disillusionment and elevating the importance of traditional personal and community relationships. In this fertile soil, a new Christian movement, widely nurtured from the grassroots rather than imposed from above, has sprung to life.

The Chinese Church and Communism

Though one of earth's oldest cultures, China for centuries seemed resistant to the Christian faith. The Nestorian missionary Alopen brought Christianity to China in A.D. 635, but with no Chinese Bible and apparently syncretistic tendencies, the church disappeared within three centuries. Franciscan missionaries reestablished a Christian presence beginning in 1294. Their converts were mainly among alien groups living in China. The faith failed to deeply penetrate the Chinese people and died within a century.

Roman Catholic missionaries in the sixteenth and seventeenth centuries saw Christianity grow to some 250,000 believers, but missionaries were later banished and persecution ensued. With the coming of Robert Morrison and other Protestant missionaries in the nineteenth century, and the move further inland by J. Hudson Taylor and others, the church grew to 500,000 Roman Catholics and 75,000 Protestants by 1900.

The tumultuous twentieth century began with the Boxer Uprising of 1900 in which perhaps as many as 50,000 Chinese Christians and many missionaries were killed. Despite persecution, through the first half of the century, the church grew and established schools and medical work.

Later, beginning in 1949, the church suffered disruption and persecution under communism. Missionaries were expelled and many Christians died. In 1966 the Red Guards destroyed the remaining visible face of the church, but believers went underground. No one knows how many Christians died, rejected the faith, or simply continued as secret believers between 1949 and 1979. China counted more than three million baptized believers when the Communists came to power. The recent resurgence shows the church was far from dead, however. Today Christians outside China are in a limited way reestablishing contact with believers not heard from for decades.

Reawakening of Chinese Christianity

In 1985 Chinese national church leaders hosted fifty non-Chinese Christians at a five-day symposium on the Chinese church. The symposium was headed up by Bishop K. H. Ting Guangxun, president of the China Christian Council and head of the Three-Self Patriotic Movement, China's officially recognized Protestant body.

Ting told his visitors of increased freedom for Christians since 1979 when the Communist government of Deng Xiaoping initiated reforms. Ting said, "A growing church [now has]. . . the freedom to worship, propagate its faith, educate its youth, live in Christian homes, [and] publish journals, books, and Bibles." Another Chinese church leader said 1.6 million Bibles have been printed in China since 1980 and are available to all believers.[7]

In a news summary of Ting's comments *Christianity Today* reported:

> China's 1979 constitution, which changed the priorities of the Communist party, deemphasized the propagation of atheism and protected religious freedom. . . . Since then nearly 3,500 churches have reopened, with new churches opening at the rate of at least one a day. He also told of 'tens of thousands of meeting points,' or house churches, that are surfacing around the country. Ting estimated China's Protestant population at between three and four million, up from 700,000 in 1949. The Catholic population is roughly equal to the Protestant population.[8]

One leader from the Three-Self Movement reported that the Chinese government no longer considers Christian faith a threat, recognizing that Christians are honest workers who help the country achieve its socialist goals. Some Chinese church leaders suspect the government is simply acknowledging that it cannot modernize China without involving the church.[9]

An example comes from Moore Memorial Church in Shanghai. Church members are specially honored at places of employment because of their honesty. When workers are needed for warehouses where valuable materials are stored, those in charge ask for Christian employees. Similarly, a pastor from Foochow says that a local newspaper frequently reports positively on church activities and that the church choir and band are used in community activities.[10]

The new freedom to practice Christianity is being felt in the seminaries as well. Early in 1985 Nanjing Seminary received 450 applications for enrollment, but could take only 50 freshmen. Twelve additional Protestant seminaries are being opened, and many informal seminaries operate. Sam Wolgemuth reports, "In Foochow, there are

50 classes of volunteers who are being trained to provide leadership for groups of Christians. These classes . . . have graduated 800 in Fukien province alone."[11]

Estimates of church growth in China vary widely. Jonathan Chao of the China Church Research Center in Hong Kong estimates thirty million Christians, or fifty million "if the border regions and secret believers are included."[12] [See Chart, page   ] Taylor and others lean toward the estimate of fifty million Chinese Christians, more than fifty times the number of believers thirty-five years ago and approximately 5 percent of the population. In addition to the many Three-Self churches that have opened since the cultural revolution ended in 1979, Taylor says an equally significant phenomenon is the springing up of "many thousands of house churches, particularly in the countryside."[13]

Today the Chinese church exists in three main groups: a somewhat troubled and fragmented Roman Catholicism, the officially-recognized Three-Self Patriotic Movement, and the newer house-church movement. House churches are growing especially in the populous nonurban areas[14] and in the southern provinces "where Christianity has deeper roots."[15]

In addition to house churches, another aspect of the new Chinese church growth especially worth noting is widespread lay leadership. These features marked Christianity in its earliest days and have been common to renewal movements throughout history.[16] They suggest that the contemporary renewal in China is among the great Christian movements in history—especially considering the sheer numbers involved.

The significance of indigenous lay leadership is underscored by James Taylor. "If anything stands out in the history of the past 35 years, it is the importance of lay witness," he says. "It is humbling to see what God has done in China without the help of any missionaries, as pastors were imprisoned and the responsibility to witness fell upon laypeople." He adds, "Laypeople are witnessing effectively for Jesus Christ without any kind of church building in which to worship."[17] G. Thompson Brown observes that in the house churches "leaders are mostly laypeople and part-time evangelists," and "many are women."[18]

Two stories are typical. One Chinese Christian reports, "Three years ago I was released from hard labour, went back to my home area, and couldn't find a Christian anywhere. We began to witness. Over the last two years we have seen 7,000 people turn to Jesus Christ. We're now making application to the government to see if they will allow us to open the former CIM [China Inland Mission] church here in the city." Another Chinese believer who was sent to a commune recalls, "When I went to that commune there was not a single Christian. The Lord sent me there as a missionary. He put me in that situation to witness for him."[19]

Why are Chinese turning to Christianity in such numbers? Based on his interviews in China, G. Thompson Brown suggests several reasons:

- Curiosity and fascination about a faith long considered taboo (which may be a part of the current interest in "all things Western")
- Disillusionment with Communist ideology since the Cultural Revolution
- Search for answers to questions of ultimate meaning
- The appeal of Christian community and belonging in a disrupted society
- The witness of Christian character

• Indigenization. The Christian faith is no longer seen as alien to Chinese ways; "the major stumbling block of foreignness has been removed."

Brown notes that "Christian worship gives an opportunity to participate in one thing not controlled by the state, as a mild and permissible form of dissent."[20]

Such factors have changed the mood and the perception toward Christianity. A retired missionary exclaims excitedly, "Before we had to go to our non-Christian friends and urge them to become Christians. Today our non-Christian friends come to us and ask about our Christian faith." A city pastor says, "Today the sheep are seeking the shepherd!"[21]

What Can We Learn?

The experience of the Chinese church under communism will be studied by many for clues as to the unique power of faith over suppression, violence, and ideology. James H. Taylor suggests seven lessons that non-Chinese Christians can learn from the Chinese experience:

1. *God's sovereign rule.* The history of the church under communism in China is a lesson about divine leadership. "We are learning the lesson of God's sovereign rule in all history—not just in church," says Taylor. The authority of God is related to the renewed stress on the kingdom, or reign of God, which we will examine in the next chapter.

2. *The indestructibility of the body of Christ.* The destruction of church buildings is not the end of the church. When genuinely rooted in the biblical gospel, the church is not dependent on buildings. Governments may close church property, but this may merely open new doors for the church's witness.

3. *The permanence of a biblical foundation.* A major breakthrough for the Christian faith in China was Robert Morrison's translation of the Bible into Chinese in the early 1800s. Morrison's translation and linguistic work have been keys to evangelizing in China ever since. By and large the Chinese church is a church long literate in the Word.

4. *The church is purified by suffering.* Persecuted for adopting a "foreign faith", and persecuted especially under communism, the Chinese church historically has shown the resilience typical of a suffering church. A pastor in Peking said, "You know, Christians who come here to worship today really mean business with God." The very opposition intended to suppress the church merely drove it to its source and its true nature as the community of God's people. Cut off from foreign personnel, structures, and funding, the church learned again to rely on the Spirit and the Word.

5. *Prayer brings growth.* "We must not underestimate the impact of prayer, worldwide, in the dynamic growth of the Chinese church," notes Taylor. He tells of a Christian sister in the Chinese city where he was born who after a month of prayer and fasting saw a long-demented woman healed. In the economy of God, growth and power are the fruit of prayer.

6. *Effectiveness of lay witness.* Much of the growth springs from putting into practice the New Testament understanding that it is the privilege and responsibility of every Christian to witness for Jesus Christ.

7. *The impact of Christian love on community life.* Public questioning of the meaning of life reveals a spiritual vacuum which the gospel is entering with new power. Disillusioned people see Christians demonstrating a practical love which works through community.[22]

Chinese Christianity and the World Church

How geographically broad and long-lasting will the current Christian renewal in China be? Will the church succumb to its own success, or be slowed either by new repression or the impact of imported materialistic values? Will the Chinese church become world-conscious and outward reaching, or exhibit the historic cultural isolationism of China? Will the world church treat the Chinese church with the respect and attention it deserves or look at it only as a newly-promising mission field?

Current developments in China and earlier historical precedents suggest that the Christian renewal and growth in China are of major historic import. While we cannot now fully comprehend or predict the many variables, it seems clear that Chinese Christianity will have a vitalizing influence on the world church. Four aspects of the influence deserve special note:

- *Chinese Christians will make up a growing percentage of the world church.* Chinese constitute about one-third of the world population, but so far make up only about 2 percent of the world church. This proportion will change if, as we expect, the Chinese church on aggregate grows more rapidly than the church worldwide.

  The Chinese church will almost certainly continue to grow and mature, even should severe persecution return. Many Chinese outside mainland China are now involved in new efforts to reach their own people with the gospel. Also, the Chinese church will gain an additional half-million believers when Hong Kong reverts to China in 1997.[23]

- *The Chinese church may contribute significantly to the building of a new social order in China.* This is certainly the hope of many Chinese Christian leaders, and the church may be strategically placed for a key role. As Raymond Fung notes, "In a highly uniform and totally authoritarian society, the only regular corporate-life experience different from what the state and its apparatus can provide, and yet accessible to the people, is the Christian church—more specifically, the weekly gathering of Christians for fellowship and worship."[24]

Clearly, any Christian contribution to the rebuilding of China will affect all of world history.

- *The Chinese church will be the source of major new vitality, leadership, and structural forms for the world church.* The combination of numbers and innovative responses under hostile conditions will ensure this. The creation of a vital church under totalitarian conditions is particularly significant. Sociologist David O. Moberg says the resurgence of the church in China, especially in the house-church movement, "may be a forerunner in *deinstitutionalizing* Christianity."

- *The Chinese church will make major contributions to the theology and self-understanding of the world church.* Much of the church's theology and thought forms historically have been dominated by Greek, Roman, and more recently European and North American cultural and intellectual traditions. Latin American liberation theology has added new dimensions. But the world church has yet to see the impact of a dynamic and relatively *new* church, rooted in one of the *oldest* and culturally richest societies on earth.

Traditionally Chinese culture has stressed the community over the individual, while the opposite has been true in European and North American society. Some of the North American church's dynamic, as well as many of its problems, trace to an exaggerated individualism—the rugged individualism of the North American frontier.

With North America being the major exporter of missionaries to the world, a strong strain of this individualism infected the North American missionary enterprise for generations. This may in large measure account for the meager success of Christian missions in such nations as India and Japan. The kind of deeply-rooted individualism described in Robert Bellah's *Habits of the Heart* has shaped not only U.S. society, but also the U.S. church.[25]

A numerically strong, spiritually dynamic, and yet culturally-rooted Chinese Christianity may provide some balance to the individualism of North Atlantic Christianity, both theologically and practically. This could help the world church of the future develop a more biblically-sound practical expression, in local congregations, of the balance between the individual and the community.

Perhaps most significantly, the Chinese church will likely make a substantial contribution to a new (or renewed) global theology of Christianity and its mission. While Chinese theologians have shown little interest in liberation theology, the Chinese church has a keen sense of the centrality of traditional Christian doctrines and of the cosmic Christ.

Bishop K. H. Ting says, "You will find Chinese Christians not only talking about the Redeemer Christ, but more now about the Cosmic Christ, the Incarnational Christ, Christ as the crown and fulfillment of the whole creative process, the clue to the meaning of creation, the

One whom we find very much talked about in the New Testament, especially in the Fourth Gospel, in Colossians and in Ephesians."26

The impact of a resurgent Chinese church will fundamentally shape the way the church comes to understand itself as a transnational, universal faith and people. As these realities of the Chinese church pass into the history and consciousness of the world church, they can enrich its understanding of what it means to be God's people in the earth today.

Estimated Growth of the Chinese Church

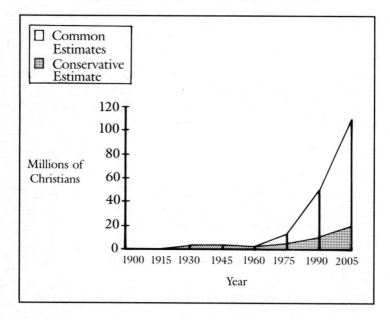

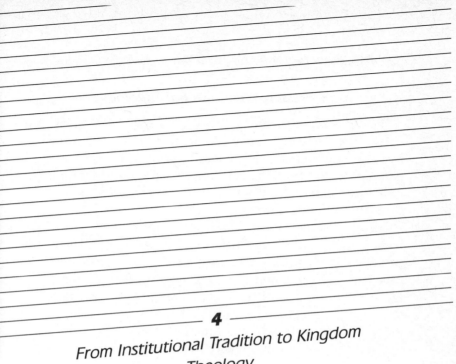

4

From Institutional Tradition to Kingdom Theology

A church embracing the entire world and touched by renewal will require a global theology, a way of understanding what God is doing today and tomorrow. As it sinks into Christian consciousness that the church envelops the whole world in actual numbers as well as in faith and promise, some rethinking of theology is inevitable. Already a trend is discernible.

The broad outlines of what may become a dominant new theology of the church are beginning to emerge. It is a theology of the reign or rule of God, a reaffirmed perception of God's sovereign direction, despite and through human agency, in the course of world history.

We look first at the theological basis of this trend and then at emerging models for the global church.

New Pressures for a Global Theology

Pressures for a theology that expands the way Christians understand the universe and their role in it come from several sources. The most important of these are internal, arising from the currents we have already traced. Others are external, arising from economic, social, scientific, and political developments.

Some of these external pressures are related to the trends projected by Naisbitt—most importantly, those from industrial society to information society, from national to global economy, and from short-term to long-term. These trends (to the degree they are in fact valid) press Christians to think in global terms, as well as to identify issues with which a functional biblical theology will have to deal in the twenty-first century.

From Industrial Society to Information Society

Most North Americans now make a living by processing information, not by producing goods. The history of the U.S., says Naisbitt, has moved from farmer to laborer to clerk. Today most workers don't plant crops or labor in factories; they handle information.

As Toffler showed in *Future Shock,* the overriding mark of modern society is the increasing pace of change. This is fed by the so-called information explosion, due in part to the growth of computer technology, which speeds up data handling. This accelerating pace of change, argues Naisbitt, makes people more future-oriented. Yet information is not the same as wisdom or knowledge: "We are drowning in information but starved for knowledge."[1]

The evidence shows that this trend itself is real enough and already is affecting church life. Three implications arise: First, the church will encounter the information handlers—these people who work with computers, data, reports, documents, and analyses. Just as farmers are different from auto assembly-line workers, so the information handlers will tend to see the world in a new way. Facing this challenge, perhaps the church will rediscover the power of the biblical gospel of true wisdom. Moving from pasture to factory to office is not, as many may think, a move away from biblical reality or God's truth.

A second implication concerns the key role of cities. Cities are storehouses of information. The modern metropolis is a complex data bank where people make their living by trading information. The key information cities of our time present a unique challenge for the church worldwide. Here the focus on urban ministry will take on new relevance and new shapes.

A third implication is the obvious question: What will the church do with all the newly available data and technology? A variety of answers is already emerging, from communications networks, use of satellites and microcomputers, and computerized data banks for church use. World Vision's Missions Advanced Research and Communications Center (MARC) for more than a decade has shown some of the possibilities in this area. Southern Baptists and other groups use computerized census analysis as a tool in church planting. Phone-linked data banks on Bible knowledge and various theological disciplines are just around the corner. Tomorrow's pastor will be able to use his or her microcomputer to search a whole library of commentaries when researching a particular verse or Bible term. Whether that will make him or her a better preacher is, of course, another question.

From a National Economy to a Global Economy

The shift to a global economy is of major significance for a kingdom theology. A factory worker on Chicago's south side tells how his plant closed when the manufacturer discovered it could make the part cheaper in Mexico City. A designer in Dearborn, Michigan, reports, "I found out what it means that Ford is a transnational corporation when the company said it would move manufacturing to other countries if workers didn't accept lower wages." These two people are beginning to understand the growing interrelatedness of the world economy and what Naisbitt calls the "global redistribution of labor and of production." The Two-Thirds World has become a major producer of goods, and now exports more manufactured goods than raw materials.

The frontier of the new U.S. economy, and the leading edge of the new world economy (according to Naisbitt and others), is biotechnology. Genetic engineering and other advances in biology and chemistry result in new industries, new products, and even a new kind of self-understanding. "Biology is replacing physics as the dominant metaphor of the society," says Naisbitt.[2] Society is moving from the machine age to the biology age.

The trend toward a global economy has special significance for the church. Christians need to think about the world in new ways. In its missions thrust, the church has come to a global awareness over the past two hundred years. And in the past quarter-century, a developing knowledge of people groups and hidden peoples has sparked new research, strategies, and consciousness. Now, instead of isolated and relatively independent countries and peoples, the world is interlaced with economic ties. In many cases these ties have become as significant in daily life as older cultural traditions were.

A missionary from North America arriving at his or her mission post today might be met by a former neighbor, transferred by General Electric or Abbott Chemicals to a new factory there. Such developments alter the whole psychology and strategy of the church—not only in missions but in the church's self-identity as God's new people or "third race" on the earth.

These issues touch not only evangelism but the church's existence as the international body of Christ in the world, called to the justice and righteousness of the kingdom on earth.

In addition, the church is learning to think of herself *organically*, rather than only institutionally or mechanically. In this respect, other cultures are well ahead of their North American or European counterparts, especially those that have never passed through the mechanistic phase of the Industrial Revolution. The emerging global economy will mean that organic and community models of the church and kingdom of God will have greatest relevance for the future.

From Short-Term to Long-Term

Naisbitt points out that the leading, innovative enterprises today are gaining the edge by learning to think and plan long-term. While this shift has not yet taken place for the majority of people or organizations, it is true of those in the vanguard. Those who learn to think long-term will have an edge over those who don't. The more dynamic enterprises today understand this.

Naisbitt says strategic planning is worthless without a strategic vision. For this reason, businesses and other enterprises are being encouraged to look at their basic purpose. "The question for the 1980s," says Naisbitt, "is 'What business are you really in?'"[3]

This question should shake the church, especially in North America. Are we in the religion business, or in the redemption business? Are we merely in church business, or are we in kingdom business? Naisbitt suggests that the railway companies in the U.S. made a fatal mistake by thinking they were in the railroad business instead of the transportation business, and many went broke as a consequence.[4]

This issue also has meaning for the church: First, the church will face the challenge of seeing herself in long-term kingdom business, not in the short-term institutional religion or even church-growth business.

Despite our sometimes careless speech, Christians cannot, of course, build the kingdom of God. God alone establishes his reign. But the church can build kingdom communities. That is, Christians can build models of the church where people really are being reconciled to Jesus Christ and to each other. This effort involves building faith communities which are as diverse as the polychrome world around us, not the monochrome congregations of yesterday where culture, race, economic status, and political views bound believers together as much as (or more than) their faith in Jesus.

Second, the church will need to develop a long-term vision and a long-term strategy for its mission in the world. This is especially critical in the areas of urban ministry, environmental concerns, social reform, and intellectual leadership. This highlights the role of Christian educational centers and such special-mission enterprises as think tanks and research centers. (The U.S. Center for World Mission is a good example of this in missions and evangelism.)

But the primary focus should be on the local church as the center of long-term vision and ministry, based on a biblical theology of the kingdom. Life in an effective church is long-term, stretching over multiple generations. The church should outsmart the world in this area, for its roots are in the biblical revelation of God who takes all of history in his view. Hence, for the church to move from short-term to long-term thinking and action is simply a matter of being more fully grounded in God's Word and less shaped by the shifting values of the world around us.

Pressures for a global theology will come from other areas as well. Major developments in science and technology will prompt Christians to develop a more comprehensive view of the world and of the Christian mission. Space flight already is affecting the way humans look at the earth. The Apollo photos of the earth, looking so beautiful and yet so vulnerable, gave many a new sense of what it means to be a part of one global village.

The next fifty years will likely see a major breakthrough in scientific understanding of the fundamental nature of the physical universe. Since Einstein's theory of relativity was published in 1915, scientists have been seeking a general Theory of Everything (TOE) which would link the four basic forces of nature: gravity, electromagnetism, and the strong and weak forces of nuclear energy. Recent string theory research by physicists worldwide may signal a breakthrough. Princeton physicist Edward Witten says the new string theory is "probably going to lead to a new understanding of what space and time really are, the most dramatic [understanding] since general relativity." "Enough beautiful things have been discovered," he says, "that we're pretty sure we've just found the tip of the iceberg."[5]

Scientific discovery and verification of a unified theory of the physical universe will have deep theological and practical implications. This will be a new Copernican revolution. It will serve to underscore the need for a plausible Christian theology of the universe—a convincing "Christian Theory of Everything" which is both biblically sound and scientifically believable. As was true of relativity, a scientific breakthrough in this area will narrow the line between spirit and matter, providing new challenges and opportunities for theology and for Christian scientists—as well as new opportunities for witness.

New Interest in the Kingdom of God

Where do Christians go for resources to define their faith in cosmic or universal terms? For many early Christian apologists it was to the Greek philosophy of Plato and others. For some Christians today it is to the ideology of Karl Marx or Adam Smith.

In the past decade, however, Christian thinkers in various parts of the world have turned to the biblical theme of the sovereign rule of God as the basic model for Christian theology in the global city. For many in North America the theme of the kingdom of God lost credibility in the wake of the fundamentalist-modernist controversy which split the holistic biblical vision into an impossible fight between the kingdom now and the kingdom future. Biblical kingdom theology was either overspiritualized (as in much premillennial dispensationalism) or largely secularized (as it is today in some liberation theology). Theologically, Marxism is a thoroughly secular-materialist version of the biblical hope of the kingdom.

A number of signs point to a renewed focus on the kingdom of God. Many books on the kingdom and related themes have been published in the last few years, and the kingdom theme is emerging with new significance in international conferences and consultations, both ecumenical and evangelical. The number of articles on the kingdom of God catalogued in *Religion Index One: Periodicals* increased from 56 in the decade 1960–70 to

139 in the decade 1970–80 (a 150 percent increase) and well over that number since 1980.[6]

The kingdom of God is such a key theme in Scripture that Richard Lovelace says, "The Messianic kingdom is not only the main theme of Jesus' preaching; it is the central category unifying biblical revelation."[7] John Bright wrote, "The concept of the kingdom of God involves, in a real sense, the total message of the Bible."[8] Peter Wagner noted in 1981 that "the kingdom of God theme had been virtually buried by American evangelicals"; it is only now being gradually resurrected.[9]

It is not possible to say where this new kingdom interest will lead, what kind of kingdom theology or theologies will emerge, or how faithful such theologies will be to Jesus Christ and the Scriptures. Some parts of the world will find kingdom terminology difficult or alienating and may opt for other terms with similar meaning. The impact of the Chinese church in this area also is not yet clear.

Biblically, the kingdom is God's rule over all he has made. This is revealed now only partially but will be manifested fully with the return of Jesus Christ. Jesus brings a new heaven and new earth filled with peace, justice, and love. He will set the whole creation free from its "bondage of corruption" and bring it "into the glorious liberty of the children of God" (Rom. 8:21), fulfilling completely all the biblical promises for an age of real *shalom* on earth.

The kingdom of God, then, looks ahead to an age and environment of peace, justice, and love analogous to but greater than that of the Garden of Eden. It will bring justice in economic, political, and social relationships, as well as ecological harmony and balance throughout the creation. God as supreme Ruler and Friend of all will be worshipped and glorified by the whole creation. Biblically, this is not an otherworldly, disembodied, nonmaterial, nonhistorical, spiritual realm of existence. Rather, it is something sufficiently like present experience that human bodies will be resurrected to be a part of it. Certainly all believers will be changed and pass into a new dimension of existence where death and the ravages of sin will be no more. This reality will come by the earth's liberation (see Rom. 8:21) through a process of death and resurrection—not by its total destruction.

Such a theology has wide-ranging implications for all areas of the church, including worship, internal community life, witness through evangelism and justice ministries, and relationship to political powers. Around these and related issues, emerging kingdom theologies will revolve.

We may expect a period of time when varying and even conflicting versions of a kingdom theology vie for acceptance as vehicles for explaining the Christian gospel. These kingdom theologies will represent different church traditions and the many national and regional contexts of the church. We do not expect or predict uniformity here. What we do think possible is a working consensus among much of the more vital and visionary sectors of the church on a kingdom theology which is biblical and communicable. It will be able to integrate creatively and redemptively such diverse concerns as the environment, sociopolitical and economic questions, spirituality and worship, missions and culture, evangelism and justice witness, as well as the problems of unity within diversity among Christians worldwide.

Of course, any number of countervailing forces could shatter a kingdom vision into irreconcilable pieces. A repetition of the great fundamentalist-modernist disaster is possible but on a much broader stage. We do not expect this, however, given the overall trend presented here. We see hope for the emergence of a sound kingdom consensus, but with many conflicting, fragmented, or reactionary theologies and movements around the fringes.

What happens theologically will depend in large measure on what happens socially and practically in the life of local congregations. It is here that new or revitalized models of the church come into the picture.

Trends Shaping Church Life

The church, as well as the kingdom, is being rethought. More organic, communitarian models of understanding the church are emerging with force and attractiveness—a development that seems to mesh with the trend from machine models to organic models in society generally. This brings us to the three additional trends that Naisbitt notes in *Megatrends*.

"From forced technology to high tech/high touch" is relevant to the quest for new models of church life. The increasing need for touch in a technical world has been one of the most mentioned parts of the *Megatrends* analysis, for it directly concerns how people relate socially. "People want to be with people," says Naisbitt, "and the more technology we pump into society, the more people will want to be with people."[10] The idea of employees sitting at home in front of their computer screens just won't happen on a large scale. People want and need human contact, especially in a technology-rich world. "We must learn to balance the material wonders of technology with the spiritual demands of our human nature."[11]

The genuine need for human touch often turns out to

be amazingly superficial—as illustrated by Naisbitt's point that the shopping mall is now the third most frequented space in the United States. Yet this trend has obvious interest for Christians. It suggests that the church must provide genuine human community. The church can offer the human touch, both in fact and in appearance. This must not be done in a manipulative way, but as an authentic expression of what the church really is in Jesus Christ—the community of God's people.

Churches need to provide community internally—in the church and in the family—and also externally in working to build community in the neighborhood. In a high-tech world, churches should concentrate on what, by grace, they can do best: build human community where people are honestly able to relate to each other with trust, confidence, and transparency.

The church will need, however, to guard against pseudocommunity. *Megatrends* reveals perhaps the greatest danger of the high-touch need today—the threat that business will move into this vacuum, creating synthetic community simply as a means toward greater productivity. This may be smart business, and highly successful, but at what cost? The need for community, which can be satisfied only through deep, committed relationships in family and church, would receive a superficial, surrogate fulfillment. Then the human touch becomes the handmaid of materialism; the way to sell more goods and services. The shopping mall becomes the church of the high-tech crowd.

The trend from hierarchies to networking is another megatrend affecting the shape of the church today in North America and globally.

Naisbitt writes:

For centuries, the pyramid structure was the way we organized and managed ourselves. From the Roman army to the Catholic Church to the organization charts of General Motors or IBM, power and communication have flowed in an orderly manner from the pyramid's top, down to its base; from the high priest, the general, the CEO perched at the very tip, down through the wider ranks of lieutenants and department managers clustered in the middle, to the workers, foot soldiers, and true believers at the bottom.[12]

Today, however, traditional pyramidal structures are being either replaced or supplemented with networking patterns, especially in the U.S. "In an information economy, rigid hierarchical structures slow down the information flow."[13] The information explosion overtaxes institutional systems, leading to more informal, horizontal, or multidirectional configurations. "The failure of hierarchies to solve society's problems forced people to talk to one another—and that was the beginning of networks," says Naisbitt.[14] Circles are replacing pyramids.

Naisbitt argues that "Networks fulfill the high-touch need for belonging." He quotes Jessica Lipnack and Jeffrey Stamps who describe networking as "appropriate sociology—the human equivalent of appropriate technology." In light of this, Naisbitt comments, "It is not the ideal time to be a traditional-type leader, either politically or corporately."[15] Or, we might add, in the church.

Networking is already a significant fact of life in the church. New or expanded networks have grown up around evangelism and world missions, urban ministry, and charismatic renewal, and around social concerns such as abortion, pornography, famine, nuclear war, and environmental pollution and waste.

One key form of networking is the linkages among intentional Christian communities and house churches, and the networking of these networks. For example, in the U.S. community networks such as the Shalom Covenant and the Community of Communities have emerged. Leaders of these and similar networks maintain contact with one another on a more or less regular basis. These linkages cover a broad range of traditions and emphases, including both charismatic and noncharismatic, Roman Catholic and Protestant, and newer and older communities. They also are becoming increasingly international.

In fact, the church itself may be seen as a network, as well as an institution. In his study of management styles, William Ouchi notes that "the traditional networks of American society" have been "family, church, neighborhood, voluntary organizations, and long-term friendships."[16] Informal and highly personal contacts have always marked the church, especially during periods of renewal, as in China.

One could argue, in fact, that the church at its most dynamic has been marked more by informal networking than by formal institutions, which usually have signaled some decline in the dynamism of the church. Students of networking might well examine the long history of the church to learn how networking functions and to understand its strengths, weaknesses, and overall dynamics. And students of the church might examine how networking can keep ecclesiastical institutions malleable.

The networking trend points toward a new conception and style of leadership. What kind of leaders will be needed in an internationalized, more organic church? We will examine this question in detail in the next chapter.

A third important megatrend is the move from representative democracy to participatory democracy. "People whose lives are affected by a decision must be part of the process of arriving at that decision," Naisbitt contends; they must "feel that they have 'ownership' in a decision if they are to support it with any enthusiasm."[17] This conviction is changing the way organizations operate and decisions are made. And the trend may be emerging worldwide.

In light of this trend, many churches will need to heighten participation in the life of the congregation. Because of the church's understandable concern with authority, leaders often tend to concentrate too much decision-making power in their own hands. To be effective in the future, churches will need to move toward wider participation, consensus decisions, team leadership, and shared vision-building.

New Models of the Church

In various ways and places the church has already begun responding to these and related trends. Examples include some of the church renewal developments in North America and Europe, the *communidades de base* or "base communities" in Latin American Roman Catholicism (as well as elsewhere), and the house-church movement in China.

In the United States, the church renewal movement has been the source of new concepts of church life. A wave of church renewal writing, especially by evangelicals, began in the late sixties and early seventies. This was fed by the cultural upheavals of the time and earlier church renewal literature from such authors as Elton Trueblood, Gibson Winter, George Webber, and Peter Berger. Other factors included the Jesus Movement, the first writings of Donald McGavran and the church growth school, and what might be styled the Personal Evangelism movement. Perhaps equally significant was the charismatic renewal which, in addition to raising the issues of spiritual gifts and community in new ways, released a new spiritual energy in the church.

Out of this ferment came such seminal books as Larry Richards' *A New Face for the Church,* David Mains' *Full Circle,* Francis Schaeffer's *The Church at the End of the Twentieth Century,* Bob Girard's *Brethren, Hang Loose!* and Ray Stedman's *Body Life.* Most of these books were more than speculation; they were linked, in one way or another, to experiments with new church forms such as L'Abri in Switzerland, Circle Church in Chicago, and Peninsula Bible Church in Southern California. They reflected renewal currents and communicated a new vision for vital church life and structures. Gene Getz gives a good summary of these developments in the revised edition of his *Sharpening the Focus of the Church.*[18]

Christians around the world operating on an organic, community model will be able to show the power of this approach, not only for international church life but for society in general. Increasing numbers of community-based churches will give support to what is already a movement in this direction. In a fascinating book, *Getting Ahead Collectively,* Albert Hirschman describes some varied grassroots programs in Latin America, many of them among church people, that illustrate how important the community concept can be to the future of both church and society.

For example, Hirschman reports that in Santo Domingo, Dominican Republic, much of the product distribution is provided by five thousand men on reverse tricycles. An iron rack mounted between two wheels in front holds the merchandise so the rider can both steer and watch his load. Most of these men are too poor to own their tricycles and must rent them for an outrageous 20 percent of their average daily earnings. Two concerned private groups developed a loan fund so the *tricicleros* could buy their tricycles on an installment plan. Since individual loans to tricycle riders would be high risk, it was required that groups of five to seven men form *grupos solidarios* and be responsible to each other to see that payment was made.

For the first time these men could own their means of livelihood. Social interaction increased between the men, and justice was served. Further:

> Once a number of *grupos solidarios* was formed, the idea arose to create a tie among the individual groups. . . . The Association soon . . . organized a rudimentary health insurance scheme and promoted contributions [to pay] . . . funeral expenses for members and their immediate family . . . . Plans are being prepared for a tricycle repair shop . . . , [and] the Association began to act as an interest and pressure group . . . . In this manner a financial mechanism originally designed to do no more than protect a lending agency against default by individual borrowers is having powerful . . . social, economic and human effects, enhancing group solidarity and stimulating collective action.[19]

Hirschman describes many similar grassroots collectives in Colombia, Argentina, Peru, Uruguay, and Chili. He writes, "Perhaps we are in the presence of a worldwide trend, for a similar movement appears to be sweeping India."[20]

These collectives are significant politically as well. Hirschman feels such organizations reinforce pluralist politics in places such as Colombia, Peru, and the Dominican Republic.

In some countries the grassroots movements and the related social activist organizations experienced sustained growth while repressive and authoritarian governments were holding power. The best and no doubt most important known case is that of Brazil with its Catholic grassroots movement known as *Communidades Ecclesiasticas de Base* (CEB). These *Communidades* multiplied in the seventies and played a significant role in the eventual "opening" of the Brazilian political system and in the partial return of that country to pluralist forms.[21]

Base communities have broad significance, both in their own right and as harbingers of new church forms. These issues have recently been explored in depth by William Cook in *The Expectation of the Poor: Latin American Base Ecclesial Communities in Protestant Perspective.*[22]

These are welcome developments and should be encouraged in the church, for the church is by definition community. This is clear both from explicit biblical references to the church as a *people, household,* and *fellowship* and from the consistent meaning of such biblical images of the church as vine, bride, priesthood, and (above all) body of Christ.

Biblically, one cannot have a church without having community. Certainly, the form and intensity of community will vary from culture to culture. Whatever the form, the following observations will increasingly apply to the church:

• *The trend toward Christian community will intensify, but will undergo change.* In many respects this trend is still amorphous and somewhat "underground." We expect new house churches will continue to be formed, intentional communities will continue to coalesce into networks, and informal networks of leaders of these various groups will maintain contact across denominational, geographic, and economic barriers. Some pioneer Christian communities such as Reba Place, near Chicago, and Sojourners in Washington, D.C., will continue to rethink and redefine their understanding of community, and some will opt for less intense forms of community.

- *A major sorting out can be anticipated in the next twenty-five years.* The church generally is experiencing a struggle between two fundamentally different models of the church. One model is organic, largely charismatic (in the biblical sense), quite informal, and to some extent communal. The other model is institutional, hierarchical, formal, and often superficial in social interrelationships.

  Given these two models of self-understanding, we will likely see more and more alliances across traditional lines of the various Christian communities. We can also expect increasing tensions between these communities and more traditional models. Christian communities may be able to exercise a mission of understanding and reconciliation throughout the whole church. At the same time, churches with little coherent inner community life will become increasingly conformed to the world and less able to communicate sympathetically with more countercultural forms of the church.

- *Relatively intensive Christian community will be seen as normative for many Christians for two reasons.* Since healthy Christian communities often have more evangelistic dynamism and more self-renewing vitality than do traditional forms of the church, more people are likely to be won and discipled through communal forms than through traditional ones. Second, the high-tech/high-touch trend is likely to predispose more people toward an informal, communitary expression of church. On the other hand, the effort and energy which often go into sustaining intense community life will in many cases act as a brake on effective ministry to the outside world.

Accurate statistics on the number of Christian groups, and information on the total number of people involved in the community movement worldwide, are not available; therefore, to date, conclusions regarding this trend are somewhat impressionistic. However, we are sure that new forms of the church are emerging in Latin America and in China. We may reasonably project that community trends within the North American church will be significantly reinforced by the broader world church.

These comments assume no significant political repression of the church in North America. The picture could change, however. Churches which stand against militarism, unrestricted capitalism or consumerism, and for human life and justice for the poor may well come under surveillance and eventual suppression by the government in coming decades. If so, the community movement might become decreasingly visible—but increasingly powerful.

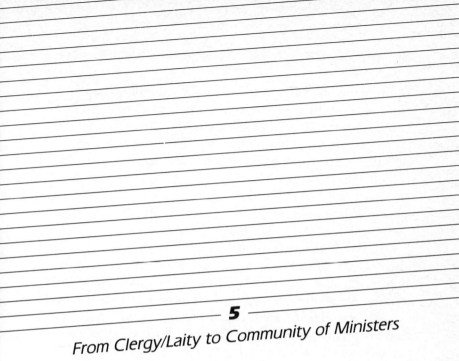

5
From Clergy/Laity to Community of Ministers

When we set out to examine the question of church leadership, we wondered whether the growing emphasis on the pastor as equipper, discipler, and enabler is a fad or a trend. Is it superficial, or does it signal fundamental changes for the church? To test this question, we listed it as a possible trend in our survey. The results are fascinating.

Overall, our respondents ranked this among the ten most significant trends. More important, respondents with greatest international knowledge and exposure considered the growth of the equipping/enabling model of leadership to be among the *five* primary trends. These observers suggest it may be a more distinct trend worldwide than it appears to be in North America or Europe.

Based on his experience with church leadership seminars in Asia and Africa, Dr. James Engel of Wheaton College reports, "The rise and growth of discipling/

equipping is the biggest and most exciting thing happening. I sense it all over the world. I find that the Lord has laid it on the hearts of pastors and church leaders wherever I go. This is a major shift, and I think it is a historic return . . . to a much more scriptural approach to the church." Engel notes further that this model is receiving new attention among such groups as the Navigators and Youth With A Mission, both of which are developing a new focus on serving the local church.

Dr. Ted Ward of Trinity Evangelical Divinity School also sees growth of the equipping model of leadership as significant, and closely related to the emphasis on community, the growth in lay ministry, and the priesthood of all believers. Historian Richard Pierard grants that this trend is significant too, but predicts, "the traditional pastor will do all he can to cling to his old authority."

The new pastoral model may indeed clash with more traditional models. Methodist theologian Theodore Runyon believes "the effectiveness of the church depends upon [this model], but institutionalism persists in American Christianity." Dr. Donald Joy puts it this way: "Original sin has power models securely in place." And Dr. U. Milo Kaufmann of the University of Illinois cautions, "The hope here is greatly tempered by my fears about the sloth of the typical churchgoer."

Rethinking Leadership Styles

New Testament Christians understood the church to be guided by the Spirit of the risen Jesus operating through "apostles, prophets, evangelists, pastors, and teachers." These were leaders whom God raised up, and who functioned organically, with the church understood as a body and the risen Christ as Head.

In New Testament days "elder" and "bishop" were equivalent terms and were understood functionally. The Greek *presbuteros* gives us the English terms "presbyter" (elder) and "priest," and the Greek *episkopos* "to oversee," the term "overseer" (bishop). Gradually the function of overseer (bishop) was separated from that of presbyter (elder). Within three or four generations a more rigid hierarchical pattern of leadership had become standard in most of the church. The functions of bishop, elder, and deacon came to be arranged as hierarchical offices. This pattern developed fairly rapidly in the second and third centuries. Thus the familiar tripartite hierarchy of bishop-priest-deacon, so common in the church for the next fifteen hundred years, was set.

With these developments, the church drifted away from team leadership (a group of elders or pastor-teachers) in each congregation to the one-man pastor over each congregation. Except in various renewal movements and some denominations such as the Plymouth Brethren, this pattern was never seriously challenged in church history until the midtwentieth century. In the light of this history, the startling significance of the trend toward a discipling/equipping model of leadership stands out sharply.

The New Testament shows that originally each Christian congregation was led by a team of spiritually mature leaders who were usually called elders. The Apostle Paul states the qualifications for such leaders in his letters to Timothy and Titus (see 1 Tim. 3:1–12, Titus 1:5–9). In his book, *The Team Concept: Paul's Church Leadership Patterns or Ours?* Bruce Stabbert shows in detail that the Bible both demonstrates and teaches plural leadership. Though many will disagree with Stabbert's assumption that elders must be male, his evidence is conclusive that plural leadership is the biblical pattern for the church.[1]

Apparently the time is ripe for a return to more biblical patterns of pastoral leadership. While so far the solid evidence is scanty, we believe a long-term trend toward the New Testament model of plural pastoral leaders is underway, and that it is becoming worldwide. We also agree that the traditional and institutional resistances to this pattern will be strong, provoking a variety of leadership situations ranging from a gradual orderly shift to the equipping model, to major controversy and splits, to a full rejection in some quarters. Speaking as a sociologist and theologian, Andrew Greeley has predicted:

> Full-time parochial clergy may diminish in relative proportion to part-time specialized or limited-term clergy, but the full-time clergy working with the local congregations will continue to be the majority of religious functionaries. . . .
> Religious institutions will no more wither away than will the Marxist state. On the contrary, they will become more elaborate and more sophisticated and more dependent on academic experts than they are at the present time.[2]

For such reasons the equipping model faces an uncertain future. But it will prove more functional in major sectors of the church around the world, particularly in cities. This is likely because of such other forces in society as the megatrends from hierarchies to networking and from representative democracy to participatory democracy. The equipping model of church leadership will probably be dominant in sectors of the church that are most dynamic, growing, and countercultural.

The Equippers

By an equipping or enabling model, we mean plural leadership whose primary function is to nurture and lead the congregation so that each believer grows and finds his or her unique function and ministry within the body. This model functions through teaching and in other ways, and may be organized in a range of culturally viable patterns. Its main principles include plurality of leadership, mutuality and consensus decision-making among the leaders, rather than top-down authority, and the enabling of all believers to exercise their particular gifts and their spiritual priesthood.

Note some of the differences between this model and the more traditional institutional model of leadership:[3]

Institutional Model	Equipping Model
Control model	Enabling model
Emphasis on authority	Emphasis on mutuality, consensus
Over/Under	Under/Up—Incarnational, elevational
Top-down process	Interactive process
Institution-centered	Person-centered
Survival-oriented	Growth/development-oriented
Program-oriented	Process-oriented
Focus on policies and programs	Focus on a climate for growth
Machine model	Organism model
Resembles Matthew 20:25	Resembles Matthew 20:26

In keeping with New Testament teachings about elders, pastors, teachers, and overseers, we see pastoral leaders having five basic functions:

1. *Prayer.* Prayer leadership is provided by both teaching and example (see Acts 6:1–4 and James 5:14). Consistent intercession for the church and for those outside the church are major concerns of leaders.

2. *Teaching/discipling.* Pastoral leaders serve as the primary teachers and preachers in the church (see Acts 6:1–4, 1 Timothy 3:2, 5:7, and 2 Timothy 2:2). Their task is to communicate the vision and direction of the church as well as to oversee all teaching, determine teaching priorities, and maintain sound biblical doctrine. Additional responsibilities are to give leadership in evangelism, in discipling new converts, and in raising up other leaders.

3. *Healing.* Matthew 10:8 and James 5:14 provide a basis for leadership in healing. This ministry involves prayer for healing of the sick or injured in body, mind, or spirit. It also includes discipling and counseling that leads to healing.

4. *Equipping/enabling others for ministry.* Ephesians 4:11–12 and 2 Timothy 2:2 show that this responsibility includes teaching and discipling believers into ministry and oversight of the church's training and discipling ministry.

5. *General oversight* (supervision). Scriptures such as Acts 20:28, 1 Timothy 5:17, Hebrews 13:17, and 1 Peter 5:2 indicate the responsibility for articulating vision, goals, and direction, and for overall administration and coordination.

C. Peter Wagner has argued that the number one vital sign "of a healthy, growing church is a pastor who is a possibility thinker and whose dynamic leadership has been used to catalyze the entire church into action for growth."[4] He admits that this may be more true in North America than in some other countries "where churches are multiplying much more rapidly than professional pastors can be trained and ordained."[5] But in North America, "the pastor has the power in a growing church"; he "is typically a strong authority figure and that authority has been earned through living relationships with the people."[6]

The pattern we are now seeing, however, is much less

authoritarian than Wagner outlines, though it does not deny legitimate authority. It is a pattern where pastoral authority is shared and where authority is linked primarily with giftedness rather than with office or position, and where the leaders freely share authority with the whole faith community—discipling and enabling everyone to exercise ministry and leadership within areas of gift and calling. This model maintains the strengths of pastoral authority but guards against its abuses through greater sharing and mutual accountability. Experience in North America and other countries has shown that this model can be dynamic both for growth and for a range of redemptive and prophetic ministries in society.

The terms *discipling* and *discipleship* have been variously understood in recent decades. In some places they have become synonymous with an overly authoritarian style of leadership which is nonbiblical and actually destructive. David Moberg notes, "Some discipling is so authoritarian that it contradicts 'freedom in Christ.'" However, Luci Shaw says discipling in the more authoritarian sense "is waning, but healthy body life should grow."

Discipling in the New Testament sense means helping all believers attain "to the measure of the stature of the fullness of Christ" (Eph. 4:13). Specifically, this is helping them to grow, to show forth the fruit and the gifts of the Spirit, and to model Jesus' life of compassionate service. Discipling in this sense is very much an equipping/ enabling function, carried on in the context of a faith community of mutual submission and mutual respect.

In our survey a number of respondents expressed doubt that the equipping model would become a significant long-term trend, given the institutional and traditional barriers against it. Some see a trend in the opposite direction, especially in North America, in light of the popularity of large churches, sophisticated techniques of planning and organization, and strong leaders. The equipping emphasis will be "countered by the large-church trend," suggests Leighton Ford.

Others noted that the model seems to be catching on here and there across denominational lines, in several Christian communities, and in such newer groups as Vineyard Fellowship, Maranatha Ministries, Agape Force, and Youth With A Mission. Though nearly all seminaries still operate on the professional leadership model, Wes Granberg-Michaelson of the New Creation Institute suggests that seminary education is beginning to be reshaped with this pattern in view.

Outside North America, we suspect this trend toward pastors as equippers may be stronger than many realize. William Cook, author of *The Expectation of the Poor,* observes that it "is a very important trend in Latin America." And the church in China is flourishing under a similar style of ministry.

The Role of Spiritual Gifts

The return to this original model of church leadership is linked to other trends already identified in this book, especially to contemporary renewal currents which stress the ministry of all believers using their gifts of the Spirit.

In the Apostle Paul's first epistle to the Corinthians we read, "There are diversities of gifts, but the same Spirit" (12:4). And in Romans, we have "gifts differing according to the grace that is given to us" (12:6).

For generations much of the Christian church has misunderstood or ignored the subject of spiritual gifts. The New Testament clearly teaches that the exercise of spiritual gifts should be part of the normal Christian life. (See 1 Cor. 12–14.) Yet even today many Christians either deny the validity of gifts by limiting them to the early church, or reinterpret them in a way that makes them synonymous with native abilities. This neglect and misunderstanding has caused some groups to overemphasize certain gifts, thus polarizing the church on the subject. Today we are seeing a new recognition by both Pentecostals and non-Pentecostals that spiritual gifts must be understood in their biblical context as part of God's plan for the healthy functioning of the Christian community.

More and more Christians today are recognizing that spiritual gifts are not a strange doctrine but one the early church understood well. In the book of Ephesians the section on spiritual gifts forms the connecting link between Paul's statement of God's cosmic plan for the church and his description of normal local church life: "There is one body and one Spirit . . . but to each one of us grace was given according to the measure of Christ's gift . . . . He Himself gave some to be apostles, some prophets, some evangelists, and some pastors and teachers" (Eph. 4:4, 7, 11).

In many places church life is seen as a community of Spirit-filled Christians exercising their spiritual gifts. Some, like Peter, Paul, Barnabas, Philip, and Apollos, used them to proclaim the gospel in the world; others to sustain the internal life of the church—as did Timothy, Ananias (see Acts 9:10), Mary the mother of Mark (see Acts 12:12), Phoebe (see Rom. 16:1–2), Priscilla and Aquila (see Rom. 16:3), and others we read about in the New Testament.

New Testament examples reflect two directions of spiritual gifts: outward (ministry in the world) and inward (ministry within the church). Both are important, for proclaiming and serving grow naturally out of the church's experience of community.

In the first epistle of Peter we read perhaps the clearest summary of biblical teaching concerning spiritual gifts. "As each one has received a gift, minister it to one another, as good stewards of the manifold grace of God. If anyone speaks, let him speak as the oracles of God. If anyone ministers, let him do it as with the ability which God supplies, that in all things God may be glorified through Jesus Christ" (4:10–11).

Clearly spiritual gifts were not just Paul's idea but were commonly accepted and understood throughout the early church. Peter assumes that each believer receives at least one spiritual gift, and that these gifts are to be used to glorify God.[7]

Many churches have shown the contemporary relevance of biblical teachings on gifts for church life and leadership. It is the collective experience of such churches which is gradually extending this trend more broadly throughout the global body of Christ.

The Pastor as Equipper/Enabler

The gifts of the Spirit connect doubly with the pastoral function in the New Testament. First, in the biblical view pastoring and teaching are spiritual gifts. At the same time these functions awaken, disciple, and direct the gift-ministries of others in the Christian community.

The pastoral and teaching ministries are distinct yet overlapping functions within the local congregation. In the New Testament, the word *pastor* did not carry the highly specialized and professional sense it does in modern Protestantism. The early church placed high priority on the pastoral *function* rather than on *office*. This shepherding emphasis is necessary for the healthy growth and ministry of the church.

Shepherding includes teaching, but the focus of the teaching is not exclusively on evangelism or on doctrinal knowledge. It focuses especially on the discipling process which leads believers into effective growth and ministry.

The New Testament concept of ministry rests on three biblical foundation stones: the priesthood of believers, the gifts of the Spirit, and servanthood in the spirit of Jesus. All believers are priests, all are gifted for ministry, and all are called to be the servants of Jesus and others. The point of leadership is to make disciples rather than perpetuating the clergy/laity distinction, which is a later historical development not found in Scripture.

Jesus said he was sending out his followers to make disciples (see Matt. 28:19). Essentially, the pastoral priority is to so invest oneself in a few other persons that they also become disciplers and ministers of Jesus Christ. In giving oneself to others in the work of discipling, the New Testament norm of plural leadership becomes a reality, as does the ministry of all God's people.

God has promised to give sufficient gifts so that through the discipling process all leadership needs are met—whether in evangelism, social witness, teaching, or any other area. According to Ephesians 4:11–16, it is only on this basis that God promises to bring the church to spiritual maturity.

Christian fellowships which are putting this model of leadership into practice are learning a pastoral theology that is functional and dynamic. This trend links in a strategic and creative way also with the new theology of the kingdom.

In the enabling model, pastoral functions are oriented to equipping God's people for kingdom life and ministry.

This is because discipling is teaching understood from the perspective of the kingdom rather than from the perspective of secular education. It is precisely what Jesus taught (see Matt. 28:20): Once the discipling priority is clear, preaching, teaching, counselling, worship guidance, and other activities serve the priority of disciple making.

Those who practice this kind of ministry will see themselves doing what Jesus did. Equipping pastors focus on developing a small group of disciples who become ministers and disciplers themselves. As pastors do this, new ministries emerge organically, and more needs are touched than even the most professional, organized, educated, or charismatic pastor could ever accomplish alone.

In the equipping model, pastoral leaders minister according to their gifts. Naturally, they also must serve carefully and faithfully in some areas where they are not gifted. This is the cost of servanthood. Though discipling is shepherding, it is more, for Christians are not sheep. They are human beings made in the image of God. Pastoring goes beyond feeding and protecting the flock to include transforming believers into priests, ministers, and servants in their own right.

In sum, the concept and general direction of this trend are clear. Less clear is how broadly it will take hold and how fundamentally it will shape the future of the church. Evidence so far suggests that this is a significant change which will shape the church as fundamentally as any discussed in this book.

Community of Ministers

If the equipping model is adopted broadly, the impact will be wide-ranging:

- *Greater practice of the priesthood of believers will result.* This biblical doctrine teaches that every Christian is a priest before God and to others because of the high priesthood of Jesus. This spiritual priesthood was stressed by Luther at the Reformation. Philip Jacob Spener's *Pia Desideria,* "Spiritual Hopes," published in 1675, is credited in large measure with launching the Pietist renewal movement within German Lutheranism. Spener's program for church renewal called for "the establishment and diligent exercise of the spiritual priesthood." According to Spener, "Not only ministers but all Christians are made priests by their Savior, are anointed by the Holy Spirit, and are dedicated to perform spiritual-priestly acts." Citing Luther, Spener argued, "All spiritual functions are open to all Christians without exception."[8] This concept proved powerful as a lever to renew the church three hundred years ago. This may happen again.

- *Emerging alternative forms of pastoral training* will accompany this trend. Dynamic, growing churches become impatient with the costly and heavily academic pastoral education provided by seminaries. Sometimes they need functional shortcuts. Pastors who see their role as equipping and discipling understand that they actually are in the work of pastoral training as they see some of their disciples demonstrate gifts for pastoral ministries.

    Dozens of informal programs of on-site pastoral training—within local churches or translocally—are springing up in North America and elsewhere. One example is The Apprenticeship School for Urban Ministry (TASUM), started by Pastor Manuel Ortiz in Chicago's northside Puerto Rican community.

Such programs often link the relational dynamic of a local church with the academic resources of a recognized college or seminary.

Somewhat parallel are the informal programs of leadership training now being practiced in charismatic and other kinds of intentional Christian communities, and the scores of discipleship training schools operated worldwide by Youth With A Mission.

- *Major reforming of seminary curricula.* A number of seminaries are offering courses in discipleship ministries, though in most cases these are elective courses added to a curriculum which fundamentally presupposes the more traditional professional clergy model. We expect that some seminaries will restructure their curricula more radically, and that new seminaries or training schools based on the equipping model will continue to spring up.

- *A practical and more organic integration of a wide range of ministries* including evangelism and justice ministries, as well as the inward ministries of nurturing believers, may be expected. As believers are equipped for ministry, their emerging variety of gifts and callings lead them into a wide and unpredictable range of ministries. This can resolve the persistent tension between evangelism and justice, or between inward and outward ministry, by providing a solution at the level of practice rather than in theory only.

For all these reasons, this trend is of fundamental significance for the shape of church life as well as for effective, transforming ministry in years to come.

6

From Male Leadership to Male/Female Partnership

Changing church leadership styles ties in with another key trend: the growing number of women entering pastoral ministry. Women have entered the U.S. work force in massive numbers in recent decades. To a lesser degree the same is happening in other parts of the world. The religious parallel to this trend is the new role of women in church leadership.

Statistics show the North American church has turned an historic corner. A shift toward women as pastoral leaders on a par with men, probably irreversible, has begun. This trend will have a profound long-range impact on the structure and function of the church of the future.

In 1970 only about 2 percent of U.S. pastors were women. By 1984 that had tripled to 7 percent—still small, but continuing to grow annually.[1] Attitudes toward women as pastors seem to be changing, and the number of women in seminary has jumped dramatically.

We estimate that by the year 2000 approximately 20 to 25 percent of pastors in the U.S. will be women, with the total possibly approaching 50 percent by the middle of the twenty-first century.

This trend is captured poignantly in the experience of Myrtle Saylor. At the age of ten, kneeling one Sunday at the communion rail, she felt called to preach. Later at home she tearfully told her father, "I'm crying because I'm not a boy." When in 1915 she applied to seminary, she was told they didn't accept women. Finally, in 1972 Myrtle Saylor Speer was granted full ordination by her denomination, the United Methodist church, though by then she had retired.[2]

Earlier Women Preachers

More than a century ago evangelical Christians in the U.S. were in the forefront of the movement for women's rights. Women preachers were not uncommon, especially in the more radical Holiness and reforming groups.[3] Post-Civil War evangelical leaders and reformers such as A. J. Gordon, Wendell Phillips, and Jonathan Blanchard (founder of Wheaton College) "championed the legal recognition of the rights of women," according to historian George Marsden.[4] Both Gordon and B. T. Roberts, principal founder of the Free Methodist church, as well as others, argued that Pentecost, "Your . . . daughters will prophesy" (Acts 2:17), gave women a new status, including the right to preach.[5] Roberts saw this issue as crucial for the long-range history and mission of the church: Had women "been given, since the days of the first Apostles, the same rights as men, this would be quite another world."[6]

Women have been prominent as pastors and leaders in

some branches of the Holiness and Pentecostal movements. One example was a small denomination called the New Testament Church of Christ which united with the Church of the Nazarene in 1908. Historian Timothy Smith observed, "The women who carried on this independent gospel work seem to have combined piety and practicality to a remarkable degree. Between revivals they maintained a normal and apparently stable family life, if the few surviving letters may be taken at face value. Their husbands joined happily in their meetings when they were near home and accepted periods of separation without much protest."[7]

Women have long proved effective as leaders in foreign missions and in church renewal movements. Examples include Catherine and Evangeline Booth of the Salvation Army, Amy Carmichael, Gladys Aylward, Ida Scudder, Kathryn Kuhlman, and Aimee Semple McPherson.[8] The rapid growth and internal strength of early Methodism in England are scarcely imaginable without the key role of women as lay preachers, class leaders, teachers, and visitors of the sick. While female church leaders have their predecessors in history, many of the earlier examples are forgotten with the passage of time.

Women's leadership often diminishes as new movements grow older and more structured. Max Weber has suggested that female leadership declines as soon as a new religious movement is stabilized.

> Only in very rare cases does this practice continue beyond the first stage of a religious community's formation, when the pneumatic manifestations of charisma are valued as hallmarks of specifically religious exaltation. Thereafter, as routinization and regimentation of community relationships set in, a reaction takes place against pneumatic manifestations among women, which come to be regarded as dishonorable.[9]

The rise of fundamentalism was also a brake on greater female leadership in the U.S. church. Judith Weidman notes that though "sectarian groups such as the Salvation Army and the Pentecostal and Holiness groups thrived on strong female leadership" a century ago, "today this heritage is almost totally lost except where it was firmly institutionalized—for example, in the Salvation Army."[10] According to Marsden, "The fundamentalist movement generally allowed women only quite subordinate roles. Apparently even in Holiness traditions the role of women in the church declined during the fundamentalist era."[11]

Fundamentalist opposition to women in pastoral roles continues strong to the present. A sizable number of U.S. Christians see women pastors as representing the invasion of secular feminism into the church. *Time* magazine notes that the conservative Concerned Women for America has now surpassed the 50,000-member Eagle Forum, led by Illinois Roman Catholic Phyllis Schlafly, as the largest counterfeminist women's organization. Concerned Women counts over 500,000 members, more than the National Organization for Women (NOW), the National Women's Political Caucus, and the League of Women Voters combined.[12]

Fundamentalists often interpret such statements as "the husband is the head of the wife" (Eph. 5:23) to mean a married woman should not work outside the home or function in a leadership role over men. In a recent move to reinforce this concept Hyles-Anderson College, near Hammond, Indiana, has introduced a bachelor's degree in marriage and motherhood to encourage women to see their primary role as child rearing.

Opposition to women as pastors is not limited to fundamentalists or conservative evangelicals, however. Sizable numbers of Christians in the Episcopal Church oppose the practice of women in pastoral leadership primarily for reasons of church tradition.

Barriers to women's ordination in major U.S. denominations began falling in the fifties. The United Methodist Church and the United Presbyterian Church, U.S.A., approved ordaining women in 1956, followed by the Southern Baptist Convention and the Presbyterian Church, U.S. in 1964, and the American Lutheran Church and the Lutheran Church in America in 1970. The Episcopal Church was the last mainline U.S. church body to accept women pastors when it approved women's ordination in 1976.[13] Still, as recently as 1970 fewer than half of all U.S. religious bodies ordained women, though the picture is changing.[14]

Walter Liefeld and Ruth Tucker summarize the current status of women in the U.S. church this way:

> In spite of the official gains women have made in the church since the mid-twentieth century, women in the 1980s continued to be in a minority in leadership positions—particularly in the evangelical churches that have grown most rapidly since the 1950s. Even in parachurch ministries, where women were theoretically granted equal status, they fall far behind their male counterparts. That has been due in part to a conservative reaction that developed not only among evangelicals but in society as a whole in the late 1970s and 1980s . . . . Seminaries and Bible colleges continued to bar women from certain exclusively male areas of study, and mission boards tightened their restrictions on women who had long been involved in extensive teaching and preaching ministries overseas. The stricter controls on women's ministries among evangelicals appear to have developed largely as a reaction to the feminist movement.[15]

The basic trend toward women's pastoral leadership continues to grow, however, despite such countermoves. The trend is fundamentally significant since it is broadly based, not confined to fringe movements in the church. It is becoming institutionalized as more denominations agree to ordain women and more women enter seminaries. For these and related reasons, the trend appears to be irreversible and long-term. And just as the secular trend toward greater women's leadership is worldwide, so is the movement toward women pastoral leadership. The role of women in China's mushrooming house-church movement is one example.

The rise of women in pastoral leadership has major implications for the family and for the church generally. What will it mean for the future of the church if in the next generations 40 to 50 percent of church leaders are women?

More Women Enrolled in Seminary

Though the trend toward increased women leadership is many-sided, its leading edge is seen in dramatic increases in women enrolling in seminary. From 1972 to 1985, the number of women in seminaries increased by 334 percent, compared to only a 41 percent increase in male enrollment. By 1980 one-fourth or more of all ordination-track seminarians in several U.S. denominations were women. This was true in the American Baptist, United Methodist, United Presbyterian, and Episcopal churches and the Lutheran Church in America. In the United Church of Christ nearly half the seminarians were women, and in the United Church of Canada the total was 42 percent.[16] In mainline seminaries generally, women increased from about 10 percent in 1970 to 25.8 percent in 1985.[17] (See charts for additional data.)

In evangelical seminaries, the number of women jumped from less than 10 percent in 1970 to 16 percent in 1983. By 1985 approximately 25 percent of total enrollment at Fuller Theological Seminary and at the two seminaries of the Christian and Missionary Alliance were women. At Trinity Evangelical Divinity School, connected with the Evangelical Free Church (which does not ordain women), about 15 percent of the seminary's 1,300 students were women.[18] Even in as conservative an institution as Dallas Theological Seminary, where generally women's ordination would not be condoned, the number of female students (all in non-pastoral programs) rose from less than 1 percent in 1977 to 8 percent in 1984.[19]

No doubt some women seminarians eventually will adopt the more traditional roles of pastor's wife, support staff, or Christian educator, but an increasing number will assume pastoral leadership roles.

Women as Pastors: Today and Tomorrow

George Barna and William McKay note, "While recent events show a decided move toward acceptance of women as full-time, professional church leaders, philosophical and practical struggles are still being waged in this area."[20]

Women going into pastoral ministry face special pressures and, at times, unique costs. Seminary training and pastoral ministry can put new strains on a marriage. One very talented woman in an evangelical seminary expresses concern about "the high level of marital casualties" among women pastors she knows. She notes that despite a husband's intellectual and theological commitment to his wife's call, "there may be a great gulf between that commitment and his daily tolerance level" of his wife's "full schedule, bedtime homework, seminary relationships, and career dreams." She sees this as a gener-

Lincoln Christian College

76718

alized problem of women in pastoral leadership. "Husbands *think* they can handle being a parishioner in their wife's church, but when it comes right down to it, it's easier to attend elsewhere or avoid the situation altogether," she says. "Personally, I'm treading carefully and slowly."

Men and Women Ordination Degree Graduates by Denomination

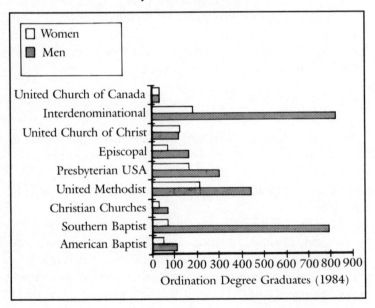

Source: Fact Book 1984-85, Association of Theological Schools in the United States and Canada

Numbers of Men and Women Graduating from Seminary

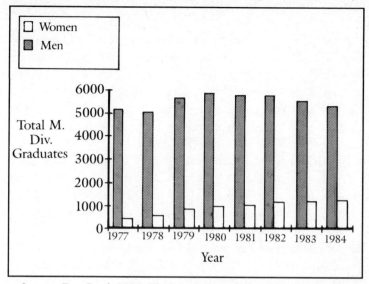

Source: Fact Book 1984-85, Association of Theological Schools in the United States and Canada

Women Enrolled in Seminary

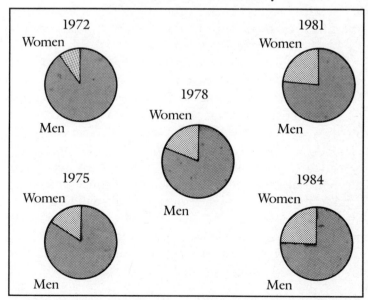

Source: Fact Book 1984-85, Association of Theological Schools in the United States and Canada

Despite struggles of this kind, women already comprise a significant minority of ordained pastors in many church bodies. By 1985, 10 percent of all Disciples of Christ pastors were women. The figure was 12 percent in the United Church of Christ, 7 percent in the Episcopal Church, 5 percent among United Methodists, and 6 percent among Presbyterians (PCUSA).

Significantly, higher percentages of women pastors have functioned for decades in several Pentecostal groups. Seventeen percent of all pastors are women in the Pentecostal Holiness Church, 12 percent in the Church of God in Christ, and 11 percent in the Assemblies of God. In general, Pentecostal and black denominations seem more open to women pastors than are other groups; one-third of female ordinations reportedly occur in Pentecostal churches.[21] A study by the National Council of Churches in the late seventies showed that of 10,470 women clergy, two-thirds belonged either to Pentecostal or "service groups" such as the Salvation Army. Nearly one-third, in fact, were in the Salvation Army where 3,037 of 5,095 officers were women.[22]

Women who have entered pastoral ministry often have done so out of a sense of divine calling. Aimee Semple McPherson tried to ignore her call after being converted as a teenager since "only men are allowed to preach," but finally obeyed what she saw as God's will. Years later she wrote, "Oh, don't you ever tell me that a woman cannot be called to preach the Gospel. If any man ever went through one-hundredth part of the hell on earth that I lived in those months when out of God's will and work, they would never say that again."[23] In 1974 Addie Davis became the first woman ordinand in the Southern Baptist Convention. The presiding pastor, though not generally favorable to women's ordination, explained. "We took her seriously when she said that God had called her to the ordained ministry and that she could not rest until she answered that call."[24]

If one considers the long-term impact women pastors will have on their congregations, and particularly on girls growing up in such churches, the magnitude of this shift becomes apparent. After initial resistance, the general acceptance of women as pastors and other church leaders on a par with men seems assured in most Protestant bodies. As resistance fades and women increasingly become pastoral role models, more and more women will probably pursue ordination.

Already attitudes toward women's leadership in the church are changing. Barna and McKay report that an overwhelming majority (82 percent) of U.S. Christians believe women should be more involved in church leadership roles, though not necessarily as pastors: "While the Christian public believes that women need an expanded part in church leadership, they are not as keen on allowing them full partnership with men in most prolific and prestigious posts."[25]

Barna and McKay conclude, "The near future will sustain the pattern of slow growth in the number of ordained women and in the levels of responsibility they will be granted," with the greatest increase coming in local "lay" leadership. They note, "Opportunities for female leadership will be especially acute in churches which are in a state of crisis . . . . The chains that have bound women to secondary functions . . . are more likely to be broken during such times of need."[26]

Women provide models of effective pastoral ministry in a variety of ways. Consider the case of Methodist pastor Elsie Johns, appointed to a "dead" city church in Michigan. When she arrived she found a welcome note on the pulpit: "There are no members and no money. Here's the key." The church building had broken windows and no heat.

After four weeks of door-to-door visits in an area many considered unsafe, not one person came to church. Finally two women came with their children, and Pastor Johns had the nucleus for a Sunday school. For fourteen years she worked part-time until the church could support her fully. In her next ten years of ministry the church grew to over one thousand members.[27]

Another example is Delia Nüesch-Olver, who as a single pastor successfully planted a Salvation Army church in an Hispanic area of inner-city Rochester, New York, in the seventies. With her husband Paul she now co-pastors the interracial, multicultural First Free Methodist Church in Brooklyn, New York, a growing inner-city congregation.

Women have not been pastoring long enough or in sufficient numbers to permit generalizations as to their effectiveness compared with men. Some studies have been made, however, of how effective men and women pastors are *perceived* to be. In one U.S. study involving 635 female and 739 male pastors in a variety of denominations, women were generally rated by their congregational lay leaders to be as effective as men. Women tended to be rated slightly higher than men in leading worship, teaching children, and involving people in ministry, and slightly lower in managing church finances. But in such tasks as teaching adults, crisis ministry, pastoral counseling, visitation, and recruiting new members, women pastors were rated equally effective with their male counterparts.[28]

Though each country presents unique features, the increase of women in church leadership appears to be a global trend. In Sweden, often considered a bellwether society for the North Atlantic nations, 10 percent of ordained priests in the Church of Sweden are women, their ordination having been approved in 1958. Women priests are now found in all thirteen dioceses of the church and account for one third of all pastors in some dioceses. One fourth of those preparing for priesthood in 1978 were women.

The Swedish situation is different from that of North America, however, as the Church of Sweden is officially linked to the government, and women's ordination was approved in part because of government political pressure. Also, church participation is low: 94 percent of the Swedish population is nominally connected to the church, but only 2 percent (excluding children) reportedly attend Sunday services.[29]

Regarding the U.S. scene, we predict that by the beginning of the twenty-first century women will be fully accepted as co-partners in pastoral ministry in most Protestant churches, with the proportion of women pastors approaching or exceeding 30 percent in many church bodies. It seems inevitable that women priests will eventually be accepted in the Roman Catholic Church as well, or in a major Roman Catholic faction which goes independent over this and related issues. A 1982 Gallup Poll showed 44 percent of North American Catholics favoring women's ordination, up from 29 percent in 1974.[30]

A Nurturing Church

What will be the long-term impact of increased numbers of women in church leadership? Our answers must be cautious, since we have no assurance current trends will continue nor any solid basis for predicting results. This, however, is what we expect:

- *The definition of the pastoral role will become broader and more flexible.* For several reasons, women will bring more variety into church leadership. Women will be the source of fresh ideas, offer different perspectives, and have a broader range of leadership styles. Eleanor McLaughlin and Rosemary Ruether think they may "by their very presence, reshape the ministry into forms that are more open, pluralistic and dialogic."[31]

  Conceptions of the pastoral role have been changing over the past several decades. The Christian ministry as a profession has often been described as in crisis. As already observed, new models of pastoral ministry arc cmcrging. Substantial increase in women pastors will strengthen the trend toward a broader range of acceptable and effective styles of church leadership.

  Some warn, however, that a long-range consequence of more women pastors may be that ordained ministry comes to be seen as a "female profession." Letty Russell comments that "ordained ministry, which is already associated with the private sphere and with feminine cultural characteristics of being loving and kind, [may] become not only 'feminized' but also 'female.'"[32] We don't foresee such a total reversal, however. In most cases men will continue to make up 50 percent or more of pastoral leadership.

- *An increase in women as pastors and other church leaders will probably strengthen the stress on community, informality, and nurture in the church.* This at least is the expectation of some women now in ministry. Dr. Leslie Andrews suggests that women's leadership will result in less emphasis on program and structure and more on nurture and the human touch. She sees increased women's leadership reinforcing the megatrend toward high touch.

Some evidence for both these points comes from a modest survey of twenty-eight churches, half pastored by men and half by women. When respondents compared the present pastors with their predecessors (all men), significant differences emerged. Women pastors were perceived as more personal in preaching, more approachable, and tended to include the congregation more in church decision-making. "In other words, the laity's perception of the shape and style of ministry does change after being served by a woman," comments Judith Weidman.[33]

- *Theologically and conceptually, more women in church leadership will increase the tendency toward organic and ecological models of the world and the church.* While generalizations can easily slide over into stereotypes, still we believe that in general women will bring the church greater sensitivity to environmental concerns, the care of the poor and oppressed, and the theological framework necessary for dealing with these matters.

- *More women in ministry will probably strengthen the trend toward lay ministry and the equipping of all believers.* Since women typically make up more than half of most congregations, the modeling of effective pastoral leadership by women should stimulate an across the board increase in women in the church's ministry. Seeing women in pastoral ministry will likely encourage women generally to use their gifts in and through the church. Dr. Leslie Andrews suggests there will be a significant entry of lay women into church leadership as they see effective models of women pastors. Whether this will mean a decline in men's leadership is an open question.

• *Church bodies which continue to restrict ordination to men will nevertheless provide expanded roles for women's leadership and ministry.* Growing recognition of women's gifts, increases in women in business and the professions, and the subtle pressure of other church bodies where women do serve as pastors will assure this.

Fundamentally the issue is not ordination or non-ordination of women but rather the issue of women participating at every level of the church. However, as participation is recognized and affirmed, in most cases it will almost certainly increase substantially. Since the ministry and leadership of women goes to the core of human sexuality, community, and self-identity, this trend will be as crucial as any in shaping the church of the twenty-first century.

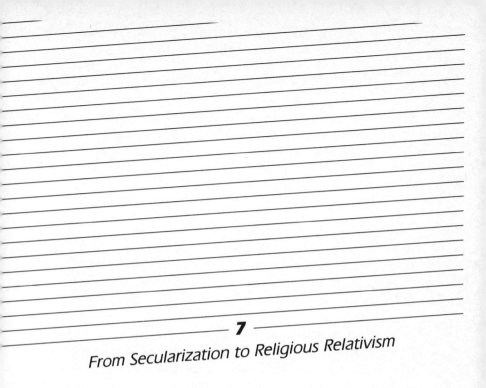

7

From Secularization to Religious Relativism

Even though it shows signs of growth and renewal, much of the church is shaped more by culture than by biblical faith. This is a key trend: the continuing secularization of the church and the rise of religious relativism.

Secularization is the process by which a relentless this-world perspective shapes all of life. David Lyon defines *secular* as "an exclusive concern with the world of the here-and-now, bound by time."[1] Religious relativism is closely linked, for in the secular view any religious perspective has validity only for those who hold it—and only because they hold it!

The church has always faced the problem of how to be in the world yet not of it. This is a constant historical pressure. But secularization comes in waves. Today the church faces a tidal wave, with many Christians in North America and Western Europe accommodating to alien values. Some surveys show little difference between the views and behaviors of those who claim to be committed Christians and those who don't.

The Secularized Church in North America

Jesus said, "If anyone desires to come after me, let him deny himself, and take up his cross daily, and follow me" (Luke 9:23). Yet many North American Christians are adopting attitudes, behaviors, and lifestyles that center more in self than service or sacrifice. We have seen the rise of what some label Christian narcissism.

In the last fifty years U.S. attitudes have largely changed from the survival mentality of the Great Depression to a drive toward self-identity and recognition as persons. Yet the understanding of the road to success hasn't changed. The survivor of the Depression sought security through good pay and financial stability. The modern "identity achiever" still follows the materialist route to reach his or her objective.

According to Barna and McKay, Christians are no different from the larger population in this regard.

> Rather than adhering to a Christian philosophy of life that is occasionally tarnished by lapses into infidelity, many Christians are profoundly secularized, and only occasionally do they respond to conditions and situations in a Christian manner. Recent research shows that many Christians are especially vulnerable to the worldly philosophies of materialism, humanism, and hedonism.[2]

This trend is seen in the rise of the prosperity gospel, which holds that material success is always God's will for believers. Christians are urged to claim, by faith, material blessings from God. Implicitly, those who are poor may have defective faith. This version of Christianity feeds on the individualism, narcissism, and affluence of North American society and largely ignores the New Testament call to follow Jesus in laying down our lives for others.

Barna and McKay report "strong support among Christians for the sixties notion that an individual is free to do whatever pleases him, as long as it does not hurt others. Two out of five Christians maintain that such thinking is proper."[3] They further note that a similar proportion of born again people deny that pain or suffering may bring greater maturity, and that 30 percent believe "nothing in life is more important than having fun and being happy."[4] These authors estimate that "less than 5 percent of the Christians in this nation are not entangled in the deceits of materialism, secular humanism, or hedonism."[5] While such terms and the supporting evidence are imprecise and subjective, many indications do point to an alarming watering down of serious Christian discipleship.

The materialism of North American Christians troubles visitors from less affluent lands. Not surprisingly, this materialism often spills over into church finances (elaborate facilities and equipment, building programs), syphoning funds from outreach and ministry programs. Narcissism and materialism make it easy for the means to an end to become an end in itself.[6]

The fitness craze that has swept North America and is now being absorbed into the church also fits the narcissistic pattern. This trend is not without its dangers. James Hunter uses the terms *narcissism* and *hedonism* in reference to the Christian's love for positive thinking, self-improvement, and a preoccupation with self, but he places Christians in a different category from the rest of the self-love folks: "The narcissism found among evangelicals is expressed not as self-infatuation or vanity or unseemly conceit and personal accomplishments. Rather, it finds expression in a fixation on the potentiality of the human being 'under the lordship of Jesus Christ.'"[7]

Yet we wonder whether this distinction is substantive or merely terminological. A possible benefit of this trend, however, is that it may lead to a search beyond fitness for wholeness—an integration of the mind, body, and spirit.

The cult of self seems well entrenched in much U.S. Christianity. "Have you noticed how natural and wholesome narcissism has become?" asks Kenneth Vaux, professor of ethics in medicine at the University of Illinois at Chicago.

> Consider the advertisements. . . . "I love my wife. She takes care of herself; exercises every day, eats sensibly, and takes Geritol every morning.". . .[This kind of narcissism] is destructive because it detroys true personhood. True personhood means being for others, not for our solitary self. The cults of humanistic psychology, ... winning friends and influencing people, composing impressive dossiers and interview demeanor—indeed, all fascinations with my own being—are depersonalizing because they intensify self-concentration.[8]

The contrast with biblical faith is put starkly by John Bright:

> Jeremiah refutes the popular, modern notion that the end of religion is an integrated personality, freed of its fears, its doubts, and its frustrations. Certainly Jeremiah was no integrated personality. It is doubtful if to the end of his tortured existence he ever knew the meaning of the word "peace." We have no evidence that his internal struggle was ever ended, although the passing years no doubt brought an increasing acceptance of destiny . . . . The summons of faith is neither to an integrated personality nor to the laying by of

all questions, but to the dedication of personality—with all its fears and questions—to its duty and destiny under God.[9]

The question before affluent Christians of the North is not whether they should be fit or well or whole but whether they are ultimately making a difference for God's kingdom. People like Jeremiah, Elijah, and the Apostle Paul remind us to ask: What does it really mean to be the people of the living God?

Much of the North American church, even that part which sees itself standing against the world, may be more massively secularized than it realizes. Historian Paul Johnson writes, "This is the first epoch in nearly 2000 years in which most governments have been guided by what might be called post-Christian ethics. And I find it to be unique in its cruelty, destructiveness, and depravity."[10]

The secularizing of the North American church may be due in large measure to the absence of persecution. George Gallup, Jr. observes:

> One can become a church member, attend church regularly, be involved in church-related activities not out of deep spiritual commitment, but out of habit, duty, or for social reasons. The fact is that while Americans regard religion as very important in their lives—the solid majority do so—relatively few say it is one of the most important influences in their lives.[11]

A Four-fold Erosion

More specifically, Gallup identifies four trends which threaten to undermine the effectiveness of the church:

1. A serious lack of knowledge about the central tenets of our religion and religious heritage;

2. An easy credulity or gullibility among North Amer-

icans that allows regular churchgoers to hold contrary beliefs (for example, on average churchgoers believe in astrology just as much as do nonchurchgoers);

3. A lack of spiritual discipline as seen, for example, in prayer life which lacks the structure, focus, and intensity required for effectiveness; and

4. An anti-intellectual tendency which promotes empty emotionalism rather than the blending of mind and heart.

From these four trends Gallup concludes that many North American Christians are highly vulnerable in their religious life and easy prey for false prophets.[12] We agree.

Consider the case of Dick and Jane Cullen, a fictitious, yet typical, young suburban couple. Dick is a realtor, while Jane works as a data processor for a Christian publishing house. Together they earn over $60,000 a year. They attend an evangelical church and consider themselves Bible-believing Christians. Last year they gave slightly more than 3 percent of their income to the church and other Christian causes, including $500 to foreign missions. Their house payment is $750 per month. They are also making payments on two late-model cars, plus a recreational vehicle which carries them away from home and church many weekends each year.

"We really believe God has blessed us," says Dick. "This is a great country, and anyone who has faith in God and works hard can prosper as we have." Partly because of this view, Dick opposes welfare payments to poor families and feels the United States must expand its military preparedness "to protect Christian and democratic values."[13]

The Cullens are typical of many thousands of North American Christians who claim a personal faith in Jesus Christ but whose lives and values mirror those of unbelievers around them more than those of Christians in other lands.

The so-called yuppie generation represents the most recent secularizing wave in North American society. The yuppie label (Young Urban Professionals or Young Upwardly-mobile Professionals) is an identity handle for the latest young hustlers and business entrepreneurs. However, this wave may be passing. At Boston University, officials are noticing more interest in liberal arts and less interest in technological and professionally-oriented fields. Admissions Director Anthony Pallett says it is too early to tell whether the seeds of a new trend have been sown, but the batch of student applications for 1985 were different than those of previous years.

"I think the Yuppie Generation is dying out, from the kids we're seeing," Pallett said. And Phillip Smith, admissions director at Williams College, a small, highly selective school in the Berkshires, agreed with Pallett's assessment. "I sense a shift away from immediate career gratification." Pallett and Smith both say they're seeing more applicants with strong social beliefs which they are willing to put into practice as volunteers in nursing homes, hospitals, and welfare agencies. "And public service is not a yuppie hallmark," Smith said. "If yuppie equals selfish, this is the other extreme."

Pallett added, "For the past ten years . . . it's been a very 'me' generation . . . . We're beginning to see a change in that. We're beginning to see an interest in causes again. . . ."[14]

If this represents a new countertrend, it could check somewhat the secular trend and reinforce those segments of Christianity calling for more radical, less compromised Christian discipleship.

In sum, the societies of the North Atlantic nations have

become largely secularized, and with them the church. The dominant, shaping values are not transcendent, spiritual, or focused on community or the common good. Materialism and affluence, institutionalized in our homes through the hypnotic eye of television, now function as the secular religion for many who consider themselves born again Christians. However, a more positive countertrend may emerge.

Countersecular Moves

Many Christians today are seeking to buttress specifically Christian beliefs (as they understand them) in various ways. The growing trend toward home education is one example. In 1984 between a half-million and a million children received in-home rather than traditional classroom instruction.[15] This indicates that many North Americans, and presumably many U.S. Christians, are rejecting at least some widely accepted cultural values and norms.

If home education is of a high quality, an additional benefit may be a new generation of well-educated Christian leaders. John Shelby Spong writes:

> The only authentic defense of the faith involves honest scholarship, not anti-intellectual hiding from truth . . . . Our scholarship ought to be so deep, so honest, and so intense that the result will be either that what we believe will crumble before our eyes, incapable of being sustained, or that we will discover a power and a reality so true that our commitment will be total.[16]

Home education, however, may not be as countercultural as it appears. Christians often exhibit a kind of sociological naiveté as to how behavior is formed. The real issue is not education (in the traditional sense) but discipling in the context of Christian community (the church). Behavior is shaped more by social contact than by information or cognitive input. Thus the most significant hope for bucking the secularizing trend may be located in the models of the church and pastoral leadership that we examined in chapters four and five.

In addition, what happens to the North American church must be viewed also in the context of developments worldwide.

Does Christian commitment in North America significantly affect daily life and behavior? Some evidence suggests it does. A 1982 Gallup Poll of more than forty questions compared spiritually committed with spiritually uncommitted individuals in the U.S. The results show the importance of Christian commitment despite secularizing. (Those considered spiritually committed believe in the divinity of Jesus Christ, say religious beliefs are the most important influence in their lives, constantly seek God's will, believe God loves them, gain a great deal of comfort and support from their religious beliefs, put them into practice, and want them to grow stronger.)

About 12 percent of the survey respondents, representing nineteen million Americans, fit the spiritually committed category. Four key aspects of their lives were strikingly different from the general population:

1. They are far happier and much more satisfied with their lot in life;

2. The divorce rate is far lower among these individuals and their families are stronger;

3. They tend to be more tolerant of persons of different races and religions than are less spiritually committed people;

4. They are far more involved in charitable activities and put a high priority on improving society.

Almost half (46 percent) of the spiritually committed respondents said they are currently working among the poor, the infirm, or the elderly. By contrast, only 36 percent of the moderately committed, 28 percent of the moderately uncommitted and 22 percent of the highly uncommitted are similarly involved.[17]

These correlations are significant. They suggest that the greater the spiritual commitment of believers, the greater their positive impact and the stronger their desire to build a sense of community in the world. If so, increasingly the dividing line in the Northern Hemisphere may be between seriously committed Christians and those who experience little more than a cultural Christianity.

Some idea of what tomorrow's evangelical Christians may be like is suggested by a survey of several hundred teens who attended a 1985 youth conference sponsored by a small evangelical denomination. Two-thirds of the group were members of the denomination. On issues of personal morality, the teens were clearly countercultural: 60 percent had never smoked a cigarette, over 80 percent had never used marijuana or drugs, and 97 percent of the girls had never had an abortion. Yet only one-third tithed regularly, and slightly more than that had daily devotions. Nearly three-fourths said they watched television two to four hours per day, and one-third had attended R-rated movies. Yet most said they wanted to improve and deepen their spiritual lives.[18]

If these teens are typical of evangelical young people, they indicate a generation with a continuing concern for personal morality but wide open to the secularizing currents of society and in great need of effective discipling.

Impact of Religious Relativism

Secularization leads either to secularism or religious relativism. The tendency among those who retain a faith in God or a religious affiliation is to compromise the unique truth claims of the faith. It becomes easy to believe: "Well, you may have your own philosophy or religion, and that's fine for you, but Christianity works for me."

In such a context, values are severed from any ultimate grounding or truth claim. They become relative and are based merely in subjective experience, whether individual or communal. Values are measured by "what works for me" or "what is right for us." Technical civilization furthers this relativism by producing an ever-expanding array of artifacts, especially material goods. In a society dominated by technique, these artifacts become the stuff from which life's meaning is constructed.

With this in mind we may ponder the megatrend that Naisbitt describes as "from either/or to multiple choice." We are moving, especially in the United States, to the smorgasbord society. "In today's Baskin-Robbins society, everything comes in at least 31 flavors," says Naisbitt.[19]

On the surface this may be simply a matter of consumer manufacturing and growing affluence, but the trend goes deeper. The varieties of toothpaste, VCRs, or specialty foods lead to a growing expectation of variety in all areas of life. One basic aspect of this tendency relates to family styles, which we will examine in the next chapter.

Accepting and expecting variety and plurality across the board are not limited to North American society. We face a worldwide trend: pluralism in religion and values rising largely from secularizing and technological influences.

The multiple-option trend means that the discipling task of the church becomes more urgent. Modern pagans are deeply embued with the idea that values—moral and otherwise—are strictly personal, having little to do with basic truths outside themselves which are valid for all people in all times. On the other hand the church, often a conservative institution, may oppose increasing variety in relatively minor matters out of fear of change, or from inability to distinguish between important and peripheral issues.

The church's discipling task will be to present and embody Christian truths without compromise while permitting greatly increased variety in areas of form and structure. On matters of right and wrong, the church must remain either/or. On matters of when, where, and how believers will meet or minister, multiple options may enhance the gospel.

Local churches certainly will have to deal with increased diversity and be customfitted to their neighborhoods instead of franchised. The medium-sized church organized like a mini-corporation and made up of stable nuclear families who drive to church on Sunday morning—the church image many middle-aged white North Americans are familiar with—is now obsolete for major segments of the U.S. population. It never was appropriate for a majority of the people of the earth.

The church will advance if today's and tomorrow's Christians can learn what it means to embody the power of the gospel, and of Christian community, in different kinds of neighborhoods and social contexts across North America and around the world. In the past the church has had her greatest impact when she found ways to authentically incarnate the gospel in different cultures and contexts. So it is today. Christians must learn to build church communities and ministries which meet the real needs of the people around them, while at the same time refusing to compromise on the truth and love of the gospel of the kingdom.

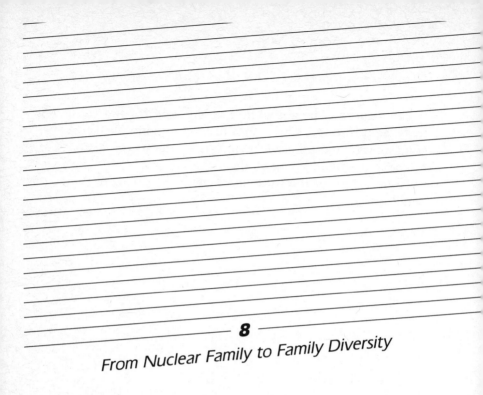

8

From Nuclear Family to Family Diversity

Near the heart of Amsterdam is a section of new apartment buildings. They are modern, but blend with the centuries-old Dutch style. A staff member of Youth With A Mission comments, "These apartments are filled with young people and many young couples. But most of them aren't married. Our neighbors are surprised when they learn we are married; marriage is just not part of the expectation or lifestyle for these people."

This example illustrates the fact that we live in a smorgasbord society where moral values vary widely. This is reflected in nontraditional family structures and other forms of human community. With growing tolerance of nontraditional family groupings, says Naisbitt, "the basic building block of society is shifting from the family to the individual."[1] A key indicator of this in the U.S. is that today one person in four lives alone, as a single person household. In 1955 the figure was only one in ten.

A 1980 study of American families noted, "The increase in the number of one-person households is a dramatic departure from most of our historical experience." The study adds, "We project by 1990 a very diverse world of households, families, and individual life histories."[2]

Naisbitt contends, "Today there is no such thing as a typical family"; and the traditional nuclear family "seems unlikely to return any time soon."[3] Only 7 percent of the North American population fits the traditional family profile of father as breadwinner and mother taking care of home and (usually two or three) children. Naisbitt says "American households of the eighties [are] a Rubik's cube of complexity. And like Rubik's cube, the chances of getting it back to its original state are practically nil."[4] He suggests the following common variations of family:

- Single parent (male or female) with one or more children;
- Two-career couple with no children;
- Female breadwinner with child and house-husband;
- Blended family consisting of a previously married couple and a combination of children from those two previous marriages;
- Unmarried couples;
- Close friends or roommates with long-standing relationships;
- Group houses where people living together have grown into a community;
- Households consisting of only one individual.

Demographers at the Joint Center for Urban Studies of MIT and Harvard published a report predicting at least thirteen separate types of households eclipsing the conventional family by 1990.[5] They suggest that the most striking change in U.S. family structure is "the decline in the share of the households headed by a married couple"—from 50 percent of new households in the fifties to only about 11 percent in the early eighties.[6]

The disintegration of traditional marriage and family patterns in the affluent nations of the North has been widely noted and commented upon. First, family size declined as economic forces, modern technology, and the move from farm to city made children economic liabilities rather than economic assets. The divorce rate skyrocketed (though it seems now to have peaked); marriage itself is questioned as moral values change; and many couples, in or out of marriage, elect not to have children. The age at which people marry has become increasingly higher, and many people are living longer—often surviving a spouse by ten or twenty years, resulting in more people living alone.

These developments in marriage and family life are fundamental. Because the family is the basic cell of society, what happens to home life affects everything else. And yet, what is true in the countries of the North is not necessarily true in the South.

Decline of the Family in the West

The decline of the traditional family is especially a North American and Western European phenomenon. It is a trend that has existed for a generation as part of the secularizing of society. Many Christians are aware of this trend and have launched a vigorous counteroffensive.

Sociologist Phillip Hammond of the University of California at Santa Barbara asserts, "A majority of Protestants are simply dissatisfied with what they regard as a moral breakdown in American society."[7] And they are not alone. Roman Catholics, Eastern Orthodox, Mormons, Orthodox Jews, and many with no religious affiliation are concerned about the morality of sixteen million abortions performed since 1973, the fourfold increase in children raised by unwed mothers since 1970, mounting drug use and child abuse, the glamorizing of promiscuity, and "gay" liberation.[8]

Clearly, we are moving into a time of increased acceptance of multiple forms of people living together, some of which Christians view as morally neutral and others as morally unacceptable (for example, unmarried couples living together and producing children). Pastors face new decisions, such as how to care for live-in couples who accept Christ. Do you marry them quickly, separate them for a time, or what? How do you bring them into the church? These ethical dilemmas are not easily resolved but are best dealt with on an individual basis.

The traditional North American church may sometimes feel ambushed by an alien culture. The people it must serve are now from many diverse cultures and traditions with greater individual freedom of choice in matters of lifestyle. By and large, white Protestant churches still assume the importance of the nuclear family (two parents, two or more children), when often that's not their primary clientele, especially in the urban scene.

John Naisbitt calls this the change from an either/or to a multiple-option society. Lyle Schaller calls it the "Big Revolution," which he defines as "the expansion of the rights of the individual and a reduction of the pressures of the culture on the individual."[9] He adds, "The emphasis is to change the culture to accommodate people and to affirm the differences among people."[10] As examples Schaller notes changes to accommodate the handicapped, changing the Army to meet the needs of volunteers, various types of "humane architecture," more female executives, and more divorces.[11]

Catering to individual tastes is increasingly evident in North America. It is perhaps best illustrated by the entertainment world. The first generation of television is credited with making America a homogeneous society. With the advent of cable and the possibility of a hundred channels comes the likelihood that the next generation will use television to reinforce individual tastes and differences. One result will be a greatly diversified society.

The increasing number of singles (both young people marrying later and older surviving spouses) provides another impetus toward an individualistic focus. Food companies respond with smaller packaging, and even new varieties of Gerbers for those wearing dentures. Residential architecture also reflects the trend toward one and two person families. We see more condos and other multifamily structures such as planned retirement communities.

The growing number of singles without traditional family ties presents a special problem and opportunity for the church. One report notes:

> There is no shortage of social and spiritual outlets devoted to singles who consider themselves Christians. Christian churches are scurrying to enlist single adults, of which there are 65 million over the age of 18, into their congregations in a move some ministers have compared in intensity with youth ministry, a concept considered revolutionary when implemented thirty years ago.[12]

Yet even within the singles subgroup there is great diversity. A 21-year-old just out of college may feel he has little in common with a 60-year-old widow or a 40-year-old divorcee. Thus many churches sponsor activities that run the gamut from field trips to amusement parks to Bible study to golf. To enhance this ministry, in April of 1985 an interdenominational group of churches formed the National Association of Single Adult Leaders (NASAL), made up of 80 members from 14 denominations representing 23 states. In contrasting church singles ministries with singles bars and other secular environments, Vi Spilker of Riverside Tabernacle in Flint, Michigan says, "Our people care about one another all week, not just on weekends."[13]

Another very important consideration in this context is the burgeoning retired population in North America. This segment has its own culture, its own values, its own gathering places, and its own migratory patterns (from the North to Florida and back). The church benefits by determining how it can minister to these individuals and also how they can minister. Special considerations are taken into account when evangelizing the unchurched of this category, and unique needs are recognized. The same planning can be effective for meeting the needs of other subcultures.

The trend from either/or to multiple option is not in itself good or bad. Diversity and homogeneity each has its place in society as well as in the church where there are "many members but one body." Even diversity in family styles is not evil provided biblical standards of morality are upheld. Single households, extended families, and shared households are viable Christian options. The challenge for the church, which in North America is often more comfortable with uniformity, will be to minister to this diversity without compromising the gospel.

The church can repackage herself to meet the needs resulting from this trend. In some circumstances the answer may be to meet in rented facilities in apartment complexes, high rises, or store fronts. This approach is common in countries of high population density such as Japan where real estate is scarce and expensive. It will be increasingly practiced in the U.S. In other cases a house church might be the right response, as in China. And there is no reason a retirement community couldn't have its own church. In any case, Christians should remember that they have as many options as the society they serve.

The Family of the Future

A poll conducted by *USA Weekend* suggests the decline of family life may be over. Interviews with 1,533 adults selected at random from across the U.S. included singles, married couples, parents, and those without children. Results showed that while two-thirds of Americans hoped to get promoted in 1986, "two-thirds would turn down a promotion that means more time away from home and children; 60 percent would refuse if it means moving."[14]

Other results of the survey are that, aside from money, parents argue most about how to discipline children (42 percent). In families with children, it was the children that brought 82 percent of parents their greatest satisfaction. And 78 percent of respondents said big family get-togethers are fun and they look forward to them. These data led the author to conclude, "One reason TV programs like 'The Cosby Show' and 'Family Ties' win top ratings: They tap our renewed interest in family."[15]

Apparently North Americans, and especially Christians, are beginning to reaffirm the importance of family. But the family of the future, however stable, will to a large extent be a hybrid, unlike anything older generations of Christians were accustomed to. The church can deal with this trend that has so dramatically altered family life if it makes adjustments.

Given the decline of traditional family structures and the fragmenting of society generally, the church will have to become a family as never before. It will need to learn in structure and practice, not just in song and theory, what it means to be the family of God, the household of Christ. The growing sense of need for "high touch" comes at a time when the most basic units for such human contact—home, neighborhood, and church—have been largely undercut or abandoned. The trend toward more women in church leadership is seen by many as a response to this need.

Today's and tomorrow's Christians face the challenge of embodying the power of the gospel, and of Christian community, in a variety of settings at our doorsteps. In the past the church's impact has been great when she has been able to adapt to changed cultural circumstances without compromising the gospel. This is the challenge again today.

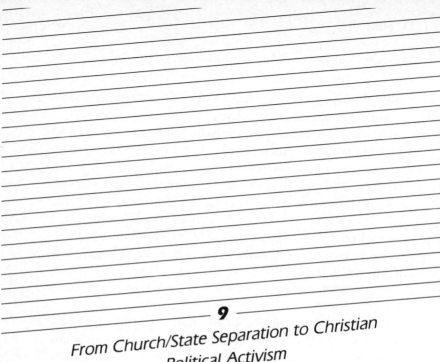

9

From Church/State Separation to Christian Political Activism

In the eighties Christians in North America entered a new phase of political involvement. The religious right, increased political activism by fundamentalists and evangelicals, and the growing number of theologically conservative Christians holding public office reflect what appears to be a new trend. Meanwhile, the "people power" revolution of Corazon Aquino in the Philippines, where the Roman Catholic Church played a key role, reveals other dimensions of Christian political activism.

Conflicting views of church and state have been with us down through church history. At one level the struggle has been between the legitimate claims and powers of political and religious authority; at another the question of how to achieve a balance between spirituality and social and political involvement. In their quest for the spiritual, monks and mystics through the ages attempted to transcend not only human affairs but the material world itself. In contrast the Roman Emperor Constantine became a Christian and saw no conflict in attempting to Christianize secular government (and in the process substantially politicized the church).

Earlier in the twentieth century conservative Protestantism, especially, tended to drive a wedge between religious experience and matters of economics and public policy. Adherents often turned inward, sharply dividing the spiritual and material realms. Yet the trend today is toward political involvement. The most visible example is the new right.

The New Right in the U.S.

The Moral Majority, founded by the Reverend Jerry Falwell, has become a potent force in the political realm. At first this group limited its activities to lobbying for such causes as school prayer and anti-abortion legislation. Evidence of their clout: The Moral Majority claims to have registered 8 million voters in the 1980 and 1984 elections. Christian Voice sent its moral-issues report cards on congressional candidates to 8 million voters in 1984. The 200,000 voters registered by the Moral Majority in North Carolina in 1984 are credited with saving the senate seat of pro-life leader Jesse Helms (even though he votes in favor of tobacco price supports for his home state).

Time magazine in its 1985 cover article on Jerry Falwell noted:

> Before Falwell, Fundamentalist preachers denounced evil in "the world" in order to compel their flocks into strict isolation from it. Nowadays those same jeremiads are a stern call to social action. "When I was growing up," recalls Fundamentalist pastor Keith Gephart of Alameda, Calif., "I

always heard that churches should stay out of politics. Now it seems almost a sin *not* to get involved."[1]

This new religious political force has considerable momentum. About 1,000 of the 9,642 radio stations in the United States now have a religious format, and a 1984 survey estimated that religious television shows are viewed regularly by more than 13 million Americans. The political message of these broadcasts are profamily and conservative.

The impact of Christian activism is being felt on the local level as well as nationally. For example, in 1980 the Reverend Marvin Rickard, pastor of the Christian Church in Los Gatos, California, organized a referendum campaign that helped repeal a local ordinance forbidding discrimination on the basis of sexual preference. One of Rickard's parishioners was elected to the city council, and in 1984 successfully sponsored a law requiring that sex magazines be placed behind opaque shields on newsstands.

Time reported that conservative, politically active Christians "get tavern hours trimmed in Anchorage; disrupt schoolboard meetings in Hillsboro, Missouri, as they demand to control curriculum; force doctors to stop performing abortions in Virginia Beach, Virginia; march in San Antonio streets to protest sex channels on cable TV . . . . The Fundamentalists 'have moved into the center of America's cultural stage,' says Baptist Pastor William Hull."[2] With few exceptions the activism of these Christians is rooted in a commitment to basic issues involving family, church, and school, but with little focus on broader issues of social justice.

Perhaps the greatest coup of the religious right to date was the election of Ronald Reagan as president. Reagan is seen as a champion of the values and rights that fundamentalists hold dear. One statistic verifying his political influence is that between 1980 and 1984 the proportion of Southern Baptist pastors who identified with the Republican party went from 29 percent to 66 percent.[3] Capturing the White House was one of many goals on the agenda for the new right. Tim LaHaye of the American Coalition for Traditional Values (ACTV) advocates that 25 percent of federal jobs be filled by Christian conservatives and thinks that "no humanist is qualified to hold any governmental office."[4]

Has the new right exhausted its momentum? Or have we seen only the beginning of a political revolution fueled by the concerns and activism of conservative Christians? We suspect the latter. Two recent developments illustrate the growing trend.

Pat Robertson, host of the *700 Club* and head of the Christian Broadcasting Network (CBN), is considering candidacy for president of the United States. Robertson is an ex-Golden Gloves middleweight boxer, an ex-combat Marine, Yale-educated lawyer, ordained Southern Baptist minister, successful businessman, and author of five best-selling books. His father was a Democrat and one of Virginia's best-known politicians, spending fourteen years in the U.S. House and twenty in the Senate. As a youth Pat Robertson rubbed elbows with the nation's policymakers, visited the White House at age 12, and later wrote campaign speeches for his father.

The A.C. Nielson Company reported that in 1985 Robertson's *700 Club* had a monthly audience of 29 million with the number growing by 30,000 per month, making it the top-rated religious show in America. And CBN now reaches around the world with 24-hour programing and has considered adding a nightly national news show. CBN employs about 4,000 people worldwide and provides an around-the-clock telephone counseling service that ministered to more than four million troubled viewers in 1985.

Besides the $22 million state-of-the-art CBN broadcast center, there is a $13 million library for CBN University. The university now offers a master's degree in five professional fields and a law school is expected to open. Another project of CBN is Operation Blessing, a philanthropic program that in 1985 coordinated the distribution of $45 million in goods and talent to impoverished people around the world. The combined ministries of CBN bring in about $230 million annually in donations and advertising. This enormous base for fundraising, grassroots acceptance, and marketing skills make a bid for the presidency a conceivable option for Robertson.[5]

Another example is the new Liberty Federation, recently established by Falwell as a parent organization for the Moral Majority. The Liberty Federation will have a bigger budget ($12 million a year, up from the Moral Majority's $7 million), and an agenda that goes beyond social issues to include foreign and defense policy. In a news conference announcing the new lobbying organization, Falwell said he wanted to back 200 conservative Christians for state and local office in 1986 and get 20 million voters of the religious right to cast ballots in the 1988 presidential elections.

"We will always be pro-family, pro-life, pro-traditional values," Falwell told reporters. "But it's time to broaden our horizons. We have found ourselves drawn into issues and conflicts which were not anticipated in 1979," when the Moral Majority was formed.[6]

The new right's broader agenda for social activism includes the issues of abortion, homosexuality, pornography, public and Christian schools, feminism, and foreign policy.

Abortion. The new right views the 1973 Supreme Court decision to legalize abortion as a declaration of war, making abortion the single most important cause of religious activists. An October 1984 Gallup poll reports 50 percent of *all* Americans (not just conservative Christians) feel abortion should be outlawed except in instances of rape, incest, or when the mother's life is in danger.[7]

Homosexuality. Motivated by a belief that government should do nothing to recognize or encourage homosexual activity, religious activists are lobbying against homosexual rights in communities across the nation. The Moral Majority repeatedly confronts the gay rights issue as part of its direct-mail fund-raising campaigns.

Pornography. Sex and violence in the press, the movies, and especially on television are seen by the new right as a major threat to religious and traditional family values. In response United Methodist clergyman Donald Wildmon initiated the National Federation for Decency. In 1982 this group boycotted television advertisers who sponsored offensive shows. More recently they are working to get the Playboy channel off local cable in many cities. Wildmon's organization also backed the picketing of 7-Eleven stores which display *Playboy* and *Penthouse* magazines, and in mid-1986 welcomed the removal of these publications from corporation-owned stores.

Public and Christian Schools. In a twenty-year period ten thousand day schools have been established. Many of these were created as alternatives to public schools where questionable books are required and where drugs, classroom violence, and secular sex education have increased rapidly. The religious schools emphasize family values, prayer and Bible study, and teachings such as creationism in addition to basic education. Their existence suggests that while religious activism has affected a few areas of government and secular life, it will be some time before public school systems are transformed sufficiently to satisfy conservative Christians.

Foreign Policy. On this issue the new right is fiercely anti-Communist and therefore favors an extensive U. S. nuclear arsenal. Their hawkish views fall under heavy criticism from many sources, and are countered by Christian passivists willing to march in protest of all forms of defense spending, nuclear and otherwise, as well as by many other Christians who question the uncritical pro-Americanism and militarism of the new right.

One area in which the church is in general agreement is in its support for the existence of Israel, although some acts of the Israeli government such as seemingly unprovoked military assaults on Lebanon and other neighbors sometimes fall under sharp criticism.

Warnings for Political Activists

As illustrated by the new right, the current trend among Christians is toward social activism with an emphasis on working to achieve justice or righteousness in society. Barna and McKay substantiate this, noting, "Survey data show Christians to be more open than non-Christians to becoming more active in community and political affairs . . . . It could well be that Christians are just waiting for someone to show them how to translate their spiritual beliefs into a practical social and political philosophy and lifestyle."[8]

Few Christians today strongly resist this trend, but many warn of inherent dangers. Barna and McKay ask,

> Should the leaders of God's people encourage believers to dive into politics? Even if the answer is affirmative . . . [leaders] will have to reflect more deeply on the relationship be-

tween Jesus' teachings and contemporary world events. Leaders will then have to communicate their perspective to believers in a manner that will educate, prepare, and motivate the flock for meaningful social action. In the process, the church must also decide whether it will continue to deny its social welfare responsibilities. If caring for the downtrodden is an accepted duty of the church, new tracks must be laid to enable the church to carry out these obligations.[9]

Others caution that if Christians are to be politically and socially involved, they must make sure they don't create problems rather than solve them. Garrett Hardin observes, "You can never do merely one thing." All actions have consequences. Often those consequences are not solutions to problems but just different problems. Thus social planning programs and other attempts at control often fail to achieve their stated goals. Schaller warns, "The more complex the situation, the more likely the intuitive response will be counterproductive."[10] Human society is part of an interdependent, organic whole, an ecological reality in which action and behavior impact everything else, even if only marginally.[11]

Another concern is that many people equate political activism by Christians as political alignment with socialism, Marxism, capitalism, or other traditional ideologies. This may be a faulty assumption. Peter Drucker has observed: "The basic issues ahead of us . . . don't fit the political alignment of the nineteenth and early twentieth centuries. They do not fit liberal and conservative and socialist. The traditional parties make absolutely no sense whatever to anybody of age 30."[12]

We are living in an age of new categories. It is no longer accurate to pigeonhole the activism of Christians on the basis of past ideological labels. The challenge for Christians will be to judge political and social activism on the basis of whether the concerns and recommended solutions make sense biblically and are workable politically.

Millennialism and Civil Disobedience

The differing views of Christians on political involvement sometimes have roots in conflicting end-time views. How does the kingdom of God in the present relate to the future kingdom?

*Post*millennialists believe the church has a responsibility to work toward God's future kingdom (the Millennium, or thousand-year reign of Christ on earth) *now*, in the present order. This optimistic view of the influence of the church-dominated early American tradition and was linked with the reforming activism of many nineteenth-century Christians. But war, disappointment, and frustrated human effort dampened this basically optimistic orientation.

*Pre*millennialists believe Christ will return before the millennium to personally inaugurate His kingdom. This sharp distinction between the current age and the future kingdom causes some premillennialists to oppose Christian involvement in politics. Other premillennialists believe Christians should promote justice in government, working not so much to establish the future kingdom as to create a political climate open to evangelism and expansion of the present kingdom (identified with the church). A. C. Dixon, editor of *The Fundamentals* (1910–1915) went so far as to encourage Christians to form political parties "for the carrying forward of any great reform."[13]

*A*millennialism is the view of the future held by many church fathers, scholastics, and reformers throughout church history. Amillennialists tend to think of the kingdom as a spiritual reality experienced in the present, or "the rulership of Christ in the world through the church."[14] They see no direct relationship between present social involvement and some future kingdom of God, though amillennialists have at times come very close to setting up their own kingdom. Calvin's Geneva is one example. And the Roman Catholic Church, which holds an amillennial view influenced by Augustine, has often shown this tendency.

Christians of varying millennial views may affirm social activism, though often with different perspectives on specific issues. For example, premillennialists have centered their social and political activism more around issues of individual or family morality than around issues of justice and reform on a broader social-structural basis. Today premillennial leaders such as Jerry Falwell, Tim LaHaye, and Pat Robertson are deeply involved in social and political issues. In addition to predictable goals, their aims include achieving justice and insuring freedom to preach the gospel.

A related issue is civil disobedience. Should Christians actively oppose or disobey the government? One premillennial analysis of Christian political involvement has been articulated by Norman Geisler of Dallas Theological Seminary. Geisler allows for the possibility of civil disobedience, based on the following guidelines:

1. Civil government is ordained by God for all people, as seen in Romans 13:1–7 and 1 Peter 2:13–14.

2. Disobedience is allowed only when government usurps God's authority such as when it: forbids worship of God (see Exod. 5:1); commands the killing of innocent lives (see Exod. 1:15–21); dictates that God's servants be killed (see 1 Kings 18:1–4); commands believers to worship idols (see Daniel 3); requires believers to pray to a

human being (see Daniel 6); forbids believers to spread the gospel (see Acts 4:17–20); and when it commands believers to worship a person (see Rev. 13).

3. There are biblical limits on how one can disobey government, and when we disobey we must be willing to accept the government-ordained consequences. Peter refused to stop preaching but did not refuse to go to prison (see Acts 5). Daniel would not pray to the king and soon found himself in a den of lions (see Daniel 6). The three Hebrew children would not bow but were willing to burn (see Daniel 3).[15]

Stephen Mott, a professor at Gordon-Conwell Seminary, has developed a somewhat more radical and elaborate biblical rationale for creative civil disobedience, not tied to any millennial theory, in his *Biblical Ethics and Social Change.*[16]

The Future of Political Activism

Whatever their motivation, Christians today are becoming involved politically in increasing numbers. We expect, as a result of this participation, that conservative moral values may be restored to some extent. This may be due to more than the direct efforts of conservative Christians. For example, Lyle Schaller notes that the sixties were unique in American history in that the population of young people had grown far more rapidly than the adult population whose job it was to civilize the youth. The result? Schaller argues that instead of being civilized by the adults, the younger generation succeeded in influencing the larger society to adopt its values. A transformation of society took place, bringing the women's liberation movement, greater racial integration, peace activism, and environmental sensitivity.

Schaller predicts that the next generation will be civilized by adults, simply because the older generation again vastly outnumbers the younger generation. Whether these individuals are Christian or not, the result will be less social unrest in America, greater stability, and "proper" socializing of young people throughout this century.[17]

Schaller's hope for a placid North American society in the next generation may be countered by new forms of unrest, and does not apply worldwide. In Mexico, the age group under twenty-five outnumbers the population over twenty-five. Also, international terrorism perpetrated on the masses by a small minority will cause turmoil. In addition to other problems, we may also experience a massive global generation gap between a graying North and a young, rebellious, and idealistic South clamoring for rights and riches now controlled by the world's affluent old folks!

Another factor that may contribute to a more conservative North American political climate is the trend to decentralize. Naisbitt describes a "new regionalism" in which "the people of this country are rebuilding America from the bottom up."[18] Pointing to increasing instances of local activism and initiative, he sees a shift of power from the central government to states and to communities. We are seeing, he says, "a huge upsurge in grassroots political activity everywhere in the United States," with activist neighborhood groups finding a new power. Often churches, he notes, are "sponsoring grassroots organizational efforts."[19]

Some question that this grassroots effort is a trend, pointing to the continuing roles of federal governmental and other centralized power sources. The analysis of this trend needs to be qualified: First, we may have two conflicting trends, one toward local initiative and the other toward more centralizing. Second, this trend may be a North American phenomenon with little parallel in other parts of the world.

A look at denominational structures shows that this trend exists in the church in North America. Nationwide denominations, even relatively small ones, report decreasing support for denominational programs and budgets, while programs and spending at local and district levels grows. In the Free Methodist Church, for instance, the percentage of giving that goes to the united ministries budget has declined steadily over the past decade, while local spending and district programs, such as camping, have spurted upward.

To the degree this trend is valid, it has at least three implications for a politically active church.

- *Local initiative and action,* while positive in many ways, *may further victimize the poor and oppressed.* In the U.S., it has been federal action in Congress and the courts which has brought greater equality for blacks and other minorities. Local majorities can be ruthlessly unjust if not accountable to powers representing a larger commitment to justice. This means the church, which often is the only voice to speak up for the poor, will need to be alert in her role of working for justice among the oppressed in society.
- *Churches often have more political power than they realize.* When society is viewed top-down, with power flowing from large, centralized institutions, the church appears weak and powerless. When viewed the other way around, however, the role of the church takes on new significance. At the local level an active, involved church can often be the glue

which holds a neighborhood together. It can be a powerful source of initiative, leavening local action in compassionate and redemptive directions rather than in the direction of mere self-protection or preservation.

- On the other hand, *small local churches often are weak and impotent in their social impact.* The need here is for local churches to strengthen their networking. This may mean strengthening denominational ties or building informal, common-interest linkages with other churches or groups which share similar concerns. For example, urban churches involved in community outreach may help each other by networking across denominational lines more than by using their own denominational connections.

Of course, there is no guarantee that the trend to decentralize will result in a more wholesome society. And not all Christian political efforts are on the side of political conservatism. Evangelicals for Social Action is a broadly-based coalition working for greater sensitivity and activism on issues of social justice, poverty, and international peace. ESA is organizing local chapters across the country. Bread for the World, another primarily Christian organization, lobbies for legislation and policies which will provide adequate food for the world's peoples. *Sojourners* magazine and the Sojourners community agitate for international justice and promote a new abolitionism against nuclear weapons. And in 1986 a new broad-based political action committee, Justlife, was formed to advocate a "consistent prolife stance," particularly on the issues of poverty, abortion, and the nuclear arms race.

The Church in Society

The politically active church of the future runs the risk of alienating the very society it is trying to transform. People today are turning their loyalties away from dependence on institutions. As Lyle Schaller noted "Institutions no longer can expect the loyalty of their constituents to be inherited by each new generation. Every organization and institution has to *earn* the loyalty of each new generation."[20]

According to Naisbitt, "During the 1970s, Americans began to disengage from the institutions that had disillusioned them and to relearn the ability to take action on their own." One result of this trend from institutional help to self-help has been the shift from a managerial society to an entrepreneurial society. Today most jobs are being created by new, small businesses rather than by large corporations. From 1969 to 1976, for example, two-thirds of all new jobs were created by businesses employing twenty people or less.

We expect this trend will influence the church in the following ways.

- The church is one of the oldest organizations of our society, and is seen by many primarily as an institution. Thus this trend translates into *a decline in the influence of the church as an institution* of authority. However, we should take a look at the genius of the church in the light of the anti-institutional trend. The best and most redemptive role of the church in society has never been as an institution, but rather as community.

  Local churches can serve as centers of initiative; as nuclei of people who, working together, can accomplish significant work for others in the world. A politically active church in this sense can be a catalyst in new ventures in housing, employment, community action, and other arenas. The success of many relatively small churches in combatting pornography in their communities provides another good example.

- The entrepreneurial explosion tends to generate considerable wealth and power for many, but also tends to sideline and marginalize those who, for whatever reason, are not able to play the game. *Entrepreneurialism is highly competitive, and it can hasten the process of the rich getting richer and the poor getting poorer.* This danger underscores the church's vital role as an advocate for the poor and marginalized in society.
- *The entrepreneurial dynamic and spirit, however, may be harnessed for evangelism, church planting, and social reform* that affirms the rule of God. Many pastors are in fact entrepreneurs. What are the possibilities for creating new ministries and enterprises that work for evangelism and justice in society?

As political involvement of Christians expands to include far-reaching issues such as foreign policy, a crucial question is whether believers can distinguish between priorities that favor God's sovereign rule and narrow nationalistic interests. This applies certainly to North American believers, but equally to Christians in places like South Africa, Lebanon, and Taiwan. The issue can be boiled down to this simple question: Will Christians be able to see, and persuade others to see, that the priorities of God's kingdom are ultimately more in one's own national interests than are narrower self-serving aims?

Any foreign policy which is bad for others cannot finally be good for us. John Briggs writes, "The most powerful nation in the world seems slow to realize that injustice and the denial of human rights are the seedbeds of revolutionary forces potentially more powerful than any the CIA can bring under control."[21] Yet in the United States the majority of conservative Christians seem consistently to support a sort of "America first" stance, which either confuses national and kingdom priorities or splits them into two unrelated worlds. A successful Christian community is one that simultaneously enables believers to be strong in faith and effectively involved in redemptive action in society.

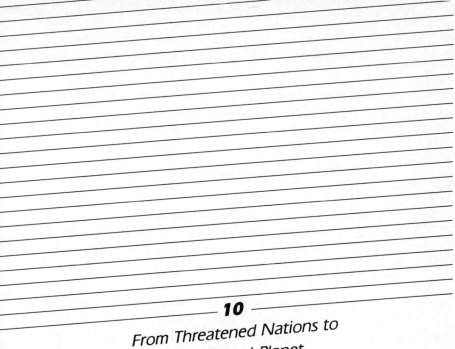

10

From Threatened Nations to Threatened Planet

*W*e began this book with a question: What trends in religion, or in society as a whole, will most affect the church in coming decades?

We have examined significant issues within the church which are of fundamental long-range import. We have concentrated on these internal issues, rather than on broader social issues and forces, because these seem most significant in the future of the church.

It would be naive, however, to ignore the broad range of social, political, scientific, technological, and economic issues which will impact the church and the world in years to come. We have noted several of these issues in passing, particularly in reviewing Naisbitt's megatrends. In this final chapter we must examine some major world trends which the church will encounter and dare not ignore. Three, especially, appear to be so basic and potentially dangerous that together they constitute megadangers for all earth's peoples. These are: the widening gap between rich and poor, our threatened ecosphere, and the dangers of nuclear armaments.

Widening Gap Between Rich and Poor

Two-thirds of the respondents to our trends survey felt that increasing economic disparity between rich and poor in the world is a key trend. About half felt it was one of the two or three most important trends. But what are the facts? Is the gap between rich and poor really widening? If so, what does this suggest?

The late Herman Kahn of the Hudson Institute in his book *World Economic Development: 1979 and Beyond,* noting "the dramatic increase in the disparity of per capita income between the wealthiest and poorest nations,"[1] said the conclusion is "virtually inescapable" that the gap between rich and poor will continue to widen over the next several decades. The goal of closing the gap between the rich and poor countries, he said, "simply cannot be approached, much less attained, in the next 100 years."[2]

Despite the politically unsettling prospects of this picture, Kahn prefers a positive assessment. The widening gap results "because the rich are getting richer," not because the poor are getting poorer. "This is not necessarily a bad thing for the poor, at least if they compare themselves with their own past or their own present rather than with a mythical theoretical gap."

Kahn therefore sees the gap as "a basic engine of growth" which "generates or supports most of the basic processes by which the poor are becoming rich, or at least less poor."[3] He adds, "The Middle-Income countries generally are in many cases closing the gap with the rich countries, but this is usually ignored in most discussions."[4]

The gap between the rich and poor nations, he says, could be closed only by a massive relocation of capital investment and consumer goods that would be politically impossible. Left alone, he argues, the gap will in time heal itself: "The widening gap is in reality a force for transferring the benefits of economic development to the poor."[5]

This analysis raises serious questions. It assumes that the widening rich/poor gap will not be so unsettling as to utterly destabilize the world politically or militarily over the next fifty years. Yet (leaving humanitarian and justice concerns aside) this is probably where the greatest danger lies. Also, Kahn's broad analysis, which lumps nations together, masks large pockets of poverty in the richer nations. It is simply a distortion, for example, to call the total U.S. population rich, or to average out the wealth in nations where a small elite class controls the vast majority of resources.

Finally, Kahn himself admits that his relatively optimistic projections could be undermined by "potentially disastrous" consequences of "bad luck and bad management," "complicated, complex, and subtle ecological and environmental issues," or other problems.[6] Thus in the final analysis the pro-gap argument comes down to this: Things probably will get better if they don't get worse. Kahn's conclusions end up being more an expression of humanistic optimism and political ideology (in essence, Reaganomics) than of reliable evidence.

However, Kahn's analysis does underscore two key facts: (1) The gap between rich and poor will almost certainly increase over the next few decades; and (2) approximately half the world's population will be neither rich nor absolutely poor, but in a middle group of relatively low and often inadequate income.

The gap between rich and poor is in large measure a matter of economic wealth and power. Today giant transnational corporations often control economic assets far greater than those of the nations where they do business. As John Briggs notes, "The existence of these powerful corporations, taken with the vast debt owed by many developing countries to the bankers of the developed world, illustrate the general maldistribution of power between the rich North and the poor South."[7] To a large degree, this is the heart of the engine which increasingly elevates the rich from the poor.

Clearly the widening gap between rich and poor, both internationally and within given societies, is one of the megadangers facing the world and the church. Where will it lead over the next fifty years? We foresee the following:

- Global public awareness of the gap between rich and poor will increase dramatically over the next two decades, probably provoking growing political unrest in poorer nations.
- Awareness also will increase in the church, where such economic disparity will become a major ethical and theological question.
- A heightened sense of solidarity between rich and poor Christians around the world will result and with it increasingly broad, effective, and sophisticated Christian efforts to share economic resources and to deal with root causes of poverty. This will lead to a deeper understanding of the New Testament concept of *koinonia*, "sharing" or "fellowship."
- This very issue also will be divisive in the church. Many affluent Christians will probably resist dealing

with it by developing practical and theological arguments against it, and may split from other Christians over the issue. This will be one factor leading to new alignments in the church.
• A result of the split between rich and poor may be new ideologies and movements (political and/or religious) which derive their energy from the tension between rich and poor in the world and which give novel or appealing interpretations to this issue.

A Threatened Ecosphere

The environment emerged as a social and political issue in the seventies. This was due mainly to new scientific discoveries on the long-term effects of pollution and the OPEC embargo with the resulting jump in oil prices. Many politicians consider environmental concern a passing fad. And funding for dealing with ecological problems has been cut drastically, especially those overseen by the Environmental Protection Agency.

It is the nature of environmental issues, however, that they don't just go away. While the oil energy crisis has passed for the moment, the longer-term problem of harnessing renewable energy sources remains. And a whole range of serious, growing environmental problems continues. Some of these are so dimly understood that to simply dismiss them could prove disastrous to human existence.

Actual or potential dangers include desertification and the destruction of arable land; the depletion of major deep-earth aquifers which provide essential water for agriculture; acid rain including widespread acidifying of fresh water lakes and the destruction of forests; the disposal of nuclear and chemical wastes; the depletion or scarcity of rare minerals essential for high-tech manufacturing; and the direct or indirect effects of genetic engineering. Related issues, scientists say, are the gradual rise of sea levels worldwide and the continuing chemical pollution of the world's large lakes such as Lake Biwi in Japan and the North American Great Lakes. These environmental issues may be political and economic time bombs, as well. Any one of them, or several in combination, could bring humanity to destruction or utter chaos.

Despite some fading of specific environmental concerns, humanity is coming to a general ecological awareness that is unprecedented in human history. The atomic bomb and the theory of relativity dramatized the interplay of matter and energy and the tremendous power packed in the atom. The growing problems of air and water pollution show the delicate balance of our ecosystem and its ultimate vulnerability. The energy crunch made us aware that earth's bounty is finite and that the key resources fueling our economic growth could run out. The dawning awareness of the economic and ecological implications of the law of entropy is raising the most basic questions about technology and progress. We have begun to think in terms of a small planet, of Mother Earth or Spaceship Earth, of a global city. Computer technology, cancer research, food studies, and other areas of investigation impress on us the intricate balance of systems and forces which make up our habitat.

We inhabit an intricate, vulnerable biosphere consisting of a few inches of topsoil and a few hundred feet of oxygen. Though the earth's peoples are finally beginning to think ecologically, it may be too late. Ecological crises have a way of sneaking up on us. We may not have enough time to make the necessary economic and lifestyle shifts to permit human life to continue past the middle of the next century.

What does potential eco-crisis mean for the future? The following appears likely:

- In the United States, the environment will re-emerge as a political issue by the turn of the century. As the long-term social and economic effects of loss of farm land and of acid rain and other forms of pollution become clear, environmental issues will again be political issues. The ramifications will be felt worldwide because of the increasing economic and communications interdependence.

- Environmental issues will continue to influence theological and philosophical reflection, furthering the use of organic and ecological models in understanding life, the world, the church, and God's work of salvation.

- Environmental issues may fuse with other concerns to bring increasing political destabilization at strategic points in the world. If the past provides clues, when resources become scarce people and nations often fight to keep what they have rather than working cooperatively to find a just solution for all. Control of the ocean's resources will be a matter of international competition and conflict.

- Knowledge of the actual ecology and environmental interdependence of the earth will increase. Assisted by computer technology and new discoveries in astrophysics, genetics, archaeology, and other fields, the delicate web of life on our planet will become clear as never before. We may hope such discoveries come in time, and that humankind will be given the wisdom and good will to use such knowledge for peace and justice. Here the church's role could be crucial.

Living With Nuclear Terror

In the documentary film "Streetwise," depicting street life in Seattle, a hopeless teenager says: "Why should I try to plan ahead? We'll probably all die in a nuclear war anyway."

What does it mean to live one's whole life under the nuclear sword? What happens to a world when it knows an atomic war could destroy all living things? The answer isn't clear, but one thing is certain: Living with nuclear terror changes the whole equation of life for millions of people. Meanwhile, events at Three Mile Island and Chernobyl have shown that the peaceful use of nuclear power may be as dangerous as nuclear arms, and that nuclear energy is a profoundly serious environmental issue.

The growing concern with nuclear power emerged clearly in the responses to our trend survey. Though the issue wasn't on our original questionnaire, it showed up strongly as a write-in observation and was incorporated into the follow-up survey.

Historian Timothy Smith of Johns Hopkins University speaks of "the dawning realization of the terror of nuclear armaments." Loal Ames of Roberts Wesleyan College warns of the "increasing polarization concerning nuclear arms." Keith Harder of the Shalom Covenant communities sees "increased armaments, especially nuclear proliferation," as a key trend.

While some psychological studies show that the nuclear threat is deeply affecting our generation subtly and unconsciously, it is often blanked out at the conscious level. Psychiatrist Karl Menninger maintains that much of the population is wearing blinders, refusing to confront the question of nuclear terror. When people do face it, he says, they expect some miracle to happen to prevent a catastrophe. Referring to a recent book, *Nuclear Holocaust and Christian Hope,* Menninger, a staunch Presbyterian, said, "The book is going to say it's terrible and it's horrible, but God will intervene. Well, God didn't intervene to save the Jews. He expects some*body* to intervene. I suppose he expects *me* to intervene."[8]

The April 1986 nuclear disaster at Chernobyl, whose full effects won't be known for years, showed that the world's over three hundred atomic power plants can themselves be nuclear time bombs. Tens of thousands of Russians received dangerously high levels of radiation, and the long-range effect on the nearby city of Kiev (nearly the size of Chicago) in uncertain.

Some U.S. scientists warn of a 50 percent chance of a similar nuclear accident in the U.S. within the next decade. Such possibilities imply major disruptions ecologically as well as economically and politically.

While it is precarious to generalize regarding the nuclear threat, we foresee the following:

- The proliferation of nuclear weapons and nuclear technology will likely continue into the foreseeable future.
- An all-out war between the superpowers is probably less likely than more limited nuclear exchanges between smaller nations. The experience and expertise gained by the superpowers from nearly half a century of restraint in the use of nuclear weapons, as well as perceived mutual self-interest in avoiding nuclear war, will probably deter a nuclear World War III.
- There will probably be at least some incidents of nu-

clear terrorism as terrorist groups or nations gain access to nuclear arms. While these may involve major bloodshed and even the destruction of some cities, their main impact will be to increase the psychological and political tension in the world.

• Major sections of the church worldwide, and possibly the majority of all Christians, may well become nuclear pacifists—with, however, a strong counterreaction from more nationalistic sectors of the church.

• Hope will be a major world question for future generations living under the shadow of the mushroom cloud. While on one hand this will be a challenge to the church, it may well open doors to a Christian gospel of hope and provide unprecedented evangelistic opportunities for biblically vital churches. For insights of contemporary relevance on this issue one could profitably study the impact of the Black Death in Europe, 1340–1350, as Barbara Tuchman has done in *A Distant Mirror*.[9]

One need not be a prophet to see that eco-crisis and nuclear terror in a world increasingly split between rich and poor, yet intimately linked by radio and television, could easily add up to a recipe for convulsions as devastating as any world war.

These issues present not a scenario for despair but simply the dimensions of the challenge we face. Europe survived the Black Death of the fourteenth century, though in some places half the population died. Floods, earthquakes, disease, and wars have threatened in the past and will do so again. Today's issues, however, are unprecedented in their scope and reach, touching the fabric of life for all earth's peoples.

From a Christian standpoint, these issues caution us against triumphalism or an easy optimism. Human sin is still with us, not only individually and in groups but cumulatively, clogging the structures of our social and environmental systems. As we move into the twenty-first century, the world is one family at war with itself and threatening to poison or explode its own home.

This is the time for the church of Jesus Christ to show that the gospel is the power of God for salvation, including redemption which reaches to the very edges of the created world. Some of the trends noted in this book give us hope, despite accompanying dangers. Christians know that realistic hope can be grounded only in God and in the provisions of grace opened to humankind through Jesus Christ. The key question comes down to how Christians respond to God's grace—by ignoring or cooperating with His grace; by turning inward to personal faith only or by incarnating a gospel as broad as the biblical vision of *shalom;* by tying religion to narrow national self-interest or by becoming an effective, redemptive global Christian community.

On these options the future of the planet rests.

CONCLUSION:
Tomorrow's Church—Alternative Futures

*T*he course of the church in the twenty-first century is not predetermined. As always the future depends on the faithfulness or unfaithfulness of God's people, the actions of those who oppose or ignore God's Word, and on God's sovereignty. Whatever the future holds, it will be shaped substantially by the ten trends traced in this book.

What about the computerizing of the church, the Ecumenical movement, the building of megachurches, and the "battle for the Bible"? As we examined our survey results, these issues did not loom as large as we might have supposed. Regarding the use of computers and other high-tech innovations in the church, respondents felt this was simply an inevitable methodological updating of little long-range significance in itself. Such technology does extend the church's ability to do either the right or the wrong thing. (See Appendix II for further survey results.)

Leighton Ford notes:

Secular futurologists are now telling us in an almost unanimous chorus that there is no positive future for mankind except through a religious transformation of human consciousness. Daniel Bell, in *The Cultural Contradictions of Capitalism,* has suggested that our civilization cannot be saved without such a rebirth of faith (though he himself is not a believer). W. W. Harmon, of the Stanford Research Institute, suggests that world society has now reached the same rock-bottom awareness an alcoholic comes to before joining Alcoholics Anonymous: it knows that it is sick and radically helpless to change; and it is ready again to call upon a power higher than itself for deliverance. What a moment for the Christian church to offer a source of courage and renewal![1]

We don't see a lot of evidence that humanity generally is near such a point of recognized need for a higher power—though certainly many individual persons and groups may be. Yet the mega-dangerous world of coming decades may lead to a more generalized sense of spiritual need.

What will life be like in 2030? The first possibility is that human life may not survive that long on earth, but we suggest four other possible scenarios.

Friendly Fascism

Bertram Gross's 1980 book, *Friendly Fascism: The New Face of Power in America,* outlined a drift toward totalitarianism in the United States based not on force but on the increasing partnership of government, business, and the military establishment. Pointing out the parallels between the rise of fascism in Germany, Japan, and Italy in the thirties and current U.S. developments, Gross warns of a new kind of fascism, "super-modern and multi-ethnic . . . , fascism with a smile."[2]

This kind of fascism in traditionally democratic societies would bring a sort of polite totalitarianism in which the church would prosper if it went along—or be increasingly squeezed if it didn't. This scenario might unfold as follows:

- An unstable economy and return to high inflation and interest rates.
- Increasing government control over the economy.
- Expanded anti-crime and anti-terrorist legislation and powers.
- Decreased tolerance of dissent and free speech.
- Surveillance and harassment of church and other groups considered to be radical or dangerous.
- Urban unrest; police state mentality toward the urban poor; decreased economic assistance and greater surveillance and control.
- Much of the church increasingly allied with the dominant political powers; discrimination against or suppression of other church groups; denial of their access to the media.
- Legal restrictions against church activities held outside church buildings.
- Parallel developments in most democratic states worldwide.
- Increasing relative importance of the church and church leaders in China and other more traditionally non-Christian lands.
- Emergence of a small but vital confessing church in the U.S.

In this scenario, much of the church would be compromised into innocuous cultural Christianity, and society generally would become repressive. But a small remnant Christian church, purified by persecution, would begin to permeate society with a leavening effect all out of proportion to its size.

Armageddon

Many conservative Christians expect a final, cataclysmic Middle East war that will spell the end of history. Events leading up to it might include the following:

• Increased military build-up by the superpowers.
• World economic monetary crises.
• Escalating tensions in the Middle East; several nations prepare to attack Israel.
• Russia moves support troops into Iran and to the Persian Gulf, attacking Iraq and gaining control of Iran's and Iraq's oil fields.
• The U.S. and allies prepare to defend Israel and Middle Eastern oil sources.
• A coalition of Arab states, supported by Russia, attacks Israel.
• The U.S. and allies send troops and weapons to defend Israel.
• Russia moves troops into Israel, and simultaneously into Cuba and other satellite nations.
• Nuclear weapons are used first in the Middle East, followed by nuclear warfare breaking out between the U.S. and Russia, leading to an all-out world war.
• Civilization as we know it is destroyed and much of the earth made uninhabitable.

This scenario would mean the end of civilized society. The church would largely disappear from the earth. Few people would survive and survivors might well be genetically damaged from radiation. This is the grimmest of the scenarios we imagine, but a possible one.

Nuclear Terrorism

A different scenario takes into account the increasing proliferation of nuclear technology and the possibility of atomic weapons being used in international terrorism. It might look like this:

- Extreme Islamic terrorists in the Middle East and/or other terrorist groups gain access to small tactical nuclear weapons.
- Nuclear blackmail results; terrorists use nuclear threats to gain political concessions.
- Major sectors of two European cities are destroyed when terrorists detonate nuclear devices; nearly a million people die.
- Nuclear panic prompts emergency measures and infringement of democratic rights in many nations.
- The U.S. and U.S.S.R. collaborate closely to contain nuclear terrorism and guard against all-out war.
- Many people turn to the church as a source of hope and security.
- The church is divided over these issues; however, an underground church emerges and grows stronger.

This scenario sees a future much like the present, but with increasing fear, turmoil, and polarization. As in South Africa today, political unrest would probably lead to repressive government action; in times of chaos nations opt for order over freedom.

These would be troubled times for the church, but might well see the beginnings of broad spiritual renewal.

World Revival

A fourth alternative sees the rebirth of the Christian church in a worldwide renewal of unprecedented dimensions. Here the major Christian renewals and awakenings of the past provide the model, viewed on a worldwide stage. The following might occur:

- Continued growth of the church in China, with increasing impact beyond China as well.

- A growing house-church movement in Russia becomes known.
- A wave of renewal sweeps the Catholic church in the Philippines in the wake of the new democratic government there and the activist role of the church; close ties and cooperation occur between Catholics and Protestants.
- Large numbers of Moslems turn to Christ, constituting a major new Christian movement.
- Secularizing trends in Europe and North America are countered by major renewal in older denominational bodies.
- Growing sense of Christian unity and solidarity worldwide, with new stress on the power and authority of the risen Christ and commitment to holistic mission.
- Church worldwide grows significantly faster than population increase.
- New Christian movements for prison reform, employment opportunities for the poor, urban revitalization, and reform of the court system.
- Emergence of effective international Christian coalitions for famine relief, food supply reform, and care of the environment.
- Emergence of strong, righteous Christian political and intellectual leaders in many nations.
- Vital Christian churches are begun in virtually every people group on earth.
- Major international agreements reached and initial steps taken toward nuclear disarmament and multilateral cooperation.

Any of these scenarios is possible, in whole or in part,

or possibly in combination. As we have stressed at various points in this book, the future finally rests on the faithfulness or unfaithfulness of the church. Perhaps this book can help sort out the issues and enable Christians to respond faithfully to the gospel of the kingdom.

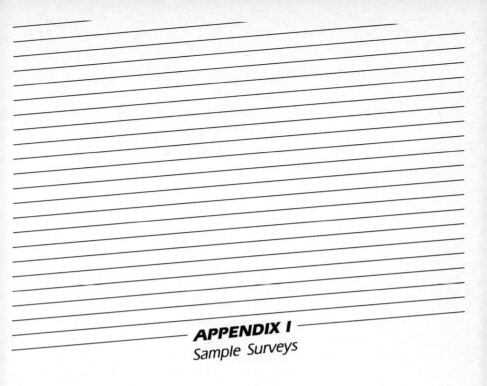

Initial Survey

TREND SURVEY: What's Ahead for the Church?

What significant trends are discernible in the church and in society today which will likely have a major long-term impact on the church? Please take a few moments to give your reactions.

Church Trends

The following 30 items *may or may not* be significant long-term trends affecting the church. What do you think? Please rate each item from 1 to 5 (low to high significance), and provide any necessary clarification or qualification. You may wish to rephrase some items. If you think the item is really not a trend or is of no future significance, place 0 in the blank.

____ 1. *Internationalization of World Missionary Enterprise;* new Third World missions agencies and structures; whole world seen as mission field.
Comment:

____ 2. *Major Increase of Women in Pastoral and Other Church Leadership;* large increase of women in seminary enrollment; relation to trend of more women in the workplace generally.
Comment:

____ 3. *Resurgence of Roman Catholic Church in World;* highly activist papacy; new Catholic orders; stress on ministry to poor rather than established power position.
Comment:

____ 4. *Growing Catholic-Evangelical Dialogue and Fellowship,* especially between evanglicals and conservative and/or Charismatic Catholics.
Comment:

____ 5. *Growing Anticipation of Major "End-Time" Religious Revival;* expectation of major revivals and renewals; growing interest in "signs and wonders" in church.
Comment:

____ 6. *Rise and Growth of Discipling/Equipping Model of Pastoral Leadership,* as compared to more traditional institutional models; questioning of traditional pastoral role; growing emphasis on equipping all believers for ministry; ministry of whole Body.
Comment:

____ 7. *Growing Interest in and Practice of Church Planting;* a number of denominations stress-

ing the starting of new congregations; many new churches being planted in U.S.
Comment:

___ 8. *Building of Megachurches;* huge local churches made up of wide variety of ministries and smaller groups and structures; both U.S. and worldwide.
Comment:

___ 9. *Growing Number of New House Churches* and related models of more intense Christian community, both U.S. and worldwide; also networking among such communities.
Comment:

___ 10. *Resurgence of the Christian Church in China,* particularly in indigenous house-church forms.
Comment:

___ 11. *Rapid Christian Growth in Third World,* particularly Central Africa and Latin America.
Comment:

___ 12. *Growing Concern With Management of Resources;* question of managing investments according to Christian principles; related stewardship and lifestyle issues.
Comment:

___ 13. *Move From Homogeneity to Diversity in Church Styles,* including in areas of worship, leadership, structure, community, and ministry.
Comment:

___ 14. *Decline of Marriage and the Nuclear Family;* high divorce rate; increasing number of single

persons and single-parent households, and of shared households, in the church.
Comment:

___ 15. *The Religious Right* in the political arena; projections of decline or continuing growth.
Comment:

___ 16. *Growing Pro-Life Activism Among Christians,* especially regarding abortion, pornography, child abuse, euthanasia, and (in some sectors) the nuclear weapons issue.
Comment:

___ 17. *Role of the "Electronic" or "Media Church";* significant level of financial and organizational resources involved; increased growth or decline?
Comment:

___ 18. *The Move Toward Christian Elementary Schools and Home Education* among many conservative and fundamentalist Christians in the U.S.
Comment:

___ 19. *A Renewed Theological and Practical Interest in the Kingdom of God* as a fundamental category for understanding the church, Christian experience, mission, and the future.
Comment:

___ 20. *Possible Increasing Government Restrictions on or Involvement in the Church* and church-related institutions; possibly leading to taxation of church property.
Comment:

___ 21. *Rise of Liberation Theologies* in Latin America

and their impact on the church worldwide.
Comment:

___ 22. *Shift in "Center of Gravity" and Major Leadership of the Church* from the U.S. and Europe to the Third World; rise of Third World Christian institutions.
Comment:

___ 23. *Rethinking of the Issue of Biblical Authority;* debate over "inerrancy" and other views of inspiration; question of normative role of Scripture in the church.
Comment:

___ 24. *The Computerization of the Church;* increasing use of computers in large church-related organizations and at local level; new software and computer information services for church use.
Comment:

___ 25. *Growing Acceptance of Abortion;* growing disregard generally for the sanctity (or unique value) of human life.
Comment:

___ 26. *Growth of the "Radical Evangelical" Wing* in the U.S. and internationally, particularly with its concern for justice for the poor and concern with peace and environmental issues.
Comment:

___ 27. *Growth and Role of "Transnational" Christian Mission and Service Structures,* e.g., World Vision, Youth With A Mission, Campus Crusade for Christ.
Comment:

___ 28. The *"Graying"* of America; increasing number of "senior citizens" leading active life; soon more people over 65 than under 18 in U.S.
Comment:

___ 29. *Growing Interest in "Fitness";* growing concern with wholeness and wellness.
Comment:

___ 30. *Growing Accommodation of Christians to Secular/Materialist Values* in their lifestyles.
Comment:

General Comments:

Which five of the above, either as listed or restated, do you consider likely to have the greatest impact on the church during the first half of the next century?
1)
2)
3)
4)
5)

Other Trends

1. What has been missed above? What other major trends *in society or in the church* do you see emerging which will strongly impact the church?
   1)
   2)
   3)
2. What significant publications or reports would you identify as especially important for this study?
3. (Optional) If you would like to respond/react to the ten "megatrends" proposed by Naisbitt, please fill out and return the enclosed additional survey sheet.

Follow-Up Survey

FOLLOW-UP SURVEY: What's Ahead for the Church?

The first 12 items below ranked highest in our initial survey (in this order). Sixteen additional items suggested by respondents have been added. Of these 28 items, which 10 do you now think are of most long-range significance for the church? Please *rank* in order of importance, one to ten (1 being most important).

____ *Internationalization of World Missionary Enterprise;* new Third world missions agencies and structures; whole world seen as mission field.

____ *Rapid Christian Growth in Third World,* particularly Central Africa and Latin America.

____ *Growing Accommodation of Christians to Secular/ Materialist Values* in their lifestyles.

____ *Shift in "Center of Gravity" and Major Leadership of The Church* from the U.S. and Europe to the Third World; rise of Third World Christian institutions.

____ *A Renewed Theological and Practical Interest in the Kingdom of God* as a fundamental category for understanding the church, Christian experience, mission, and the future.

____ *Growing Anticipation of Major "End-Time" Religious Revival;* expectation of major revivals and renewals; growing interest in "signs and wonders" in church.

____ *Major Increase of Women in Pastoral and Other Church Leadership;* large increase of women in seminary enrollment; relation to trend of more women in the workplace generally.

_____ *Decline of Marriage and the Nuclear Family;* high divorce rate; increasing number of single persons and single-parent households, and of shared households, in the church.

_____ *Resurgence of Roman Catholic Church in World;* highly activist papacy; new Catholic orders; stress on ministry to poor rather than established power position.

_____ *Resurgence of the Christian Church in China,* particularly in indigenous house-church forms.

_____ *Rise and Growth of Discipling/Equipping Model of Pastoral Leadership,* as compared to more traditional institutional models; questioning of traditional pastoral role; growing emphasis on equipping all believers for ministry; ministry of whole Body.

_____ *Growing Pro-Life Activism Among Christians,* especially regarding abortion, pornography, child abuse, euthanasia, and (in some sectors) the nuclear weapons issue.

_____ *Increasing Economic Disparity Between Rich and Poor* in the world; also in the U.S., with the "probable emergence of a new permanent underclass."

_____ *Decline of the U.S. as an Economy and Standard-Setter for World;* long-range impact of budget deficits in this connection.

_____ *Dawning Realization of the Terror of Nuclear Armaments.*

_____ *Growth of the Pentecostal/Charismatic Sector of the Church;* potential increase to 20 to 50 percent of all Christians in the world.

_____ *Growing Religious Pluralism;* relativization of world views; impact of this on the church; "need for re-stating the uniqueness of Christ in a pluralistic world."

___ *Church Unity Efforts;* e.g., Lutherans, Presbyterians, COCU, in U.S.; "increased ecumenical coopera-tion among mainline Protestant churches"; "Growing emphasis on Christian unity as con-dition/expression of renewal."

___ *Growing Emphasis on Evangelical Renewal Within Mainline Denominations in U.S.*

___ *Growing Spiritual Paganism;* e.g., "New Age," "New Consciousness" movements; quest for "spiritual" answers; increasing interest in the occult; growth of spiritism.

___ *Coalition of Christians From Various Traditions Committed to Radical Social Change.*

___ *Realignment/Restructuring of Churches* based on radical Christian/cultural religion division; declin-ing importance of denominationalism.

___ *Increased Disillusionment with Religion and Re-ligious Institutions.*

___ *"New Idolatry" of Selfism,* obsession with self-actu-alization, image, etc.

___ *Increasing Stress on Community in the Church;* em-phasis on Christian community life; understand-ing church as organic community rather than as institution.

___ *"Power Evangelism" with Signs and Wonders.*

___ *Growth in Lay Ministry;* "stronger lay participa-tion"; growing stress on priesthood of all believers as basis for ministry.

___ *Evangelicals Embracing Liturgical Worship Patterns;* increasing interest in and use of historical liturgies; growing centrality of the Eucharist for many evangelicals.

Comments:

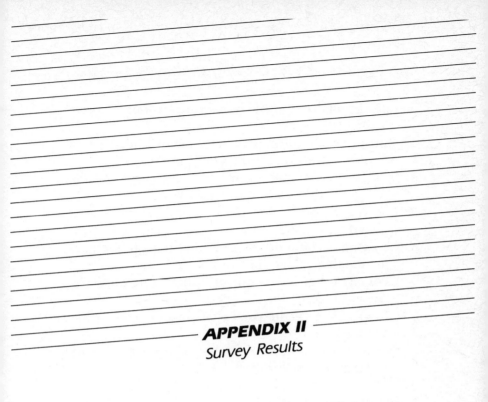

APPENDIX II
Survey Results

Here are the results of the two surveys conducted in preparation for this book. Thirty-eight people responded to the follow-up survey (including a few additional persons who did not receive the initial survey). The thirty-eight responses yielded the following ranking of twenty-eight possible trends.

Since some trends were closely related (for example, numbers one, two, and three), we have in several cases combined related trends into one chapter. In fact, most of the trends suggested by respondents are commented upon at some point in the book.

Ranking of Trends by Thirty-Eight Respondents

1. Rapid Christian growth in the Third World (210 points).

2. Internationalization of the world missionary enterprise (193).
3. Shift in "center of gravity" and major leadership of
   the church to the Third World (163).
4. Increasing economic disparity between rich and poor
   in the world and in the U.S. (153).
5. A renewed theological and practical interest in the
   kingdom of God (139).
6. Growing accommodation of Christians to secular,
   materialist values (131).
7. Growing religious pluralism; relativizing of world
   views (112).
8. Growth of the pentecostal-charismatic sector of the
   church (107).
9. Rise and growth of the discipling/equipping model of
   pastoral leadership (98).
10. Decline of marriage and the nuclear family (88).
11. Major increase of women in church and pastoral
    leadership (86).
12. Resurgence of the Roman Catholic church in the
    world (77).
13. Dawning realization of the terror of nuclear arma-
    ments (69).
14. Resurgence of the Christian church in China (56).
15. Growing pro-life activism among Christians (51).
16. Increasing stress on community in the church (50).
17. The new idolatry of selfism (49).
18. Growing spiritual paganism; interest in the occult,
    etc. (46).
19. Decline of the U.S. as an economy and standard-
    setter for the world (41).
20. Coalition of Christians committed to radical social
    change (41).
21. Growth in lay ministry in the church (38).

22. Growing emphasis on evangelical renewal within mainline denominations (36).
23. Increased disillusionment with religion and religious institutions (29).
24. "Power evangelism" with signs and wonders (20).
25. Growing anticipation of major end-time religious revival (17).
26. Realignment and restructuring of churches based on a radical/cultural division (16).
27. Church unity efforts (15).
28. Evangelicals embracing liturgical worship patterns (14).

Primary attention has been given to the fourteen items ranking highest on this list. However, in some cases the larger trends linked with specific items ranking further down in the list. We felt anticipation of major revival required a separate chapter, even though by itself it did not rank high on the follow-up survey list. In the initial survey it ranked sixth out of 30 possible trends, and its possibility reinforces some of the other trends.

Notes

Introduction

1. John Naisbitt, *Megatrends* (New York: Warner Books, Inc., 1982, 1984), 73.
2. Ibid., 1–2.
3. Jaroslav Pelikan, *Jesus through the Centuries: His Place in the History of Culture* (New Haven, Conn.: Yale University Press, 1985), 1.

Chapter 1

1. Robin Keeley, ed., *Christianity: A World Faith* (Herts, England: Lion Publishing, 1985), 5.
2. David B. Barrett, ed., *World Christian Encyclopedia: A Comparative Study of Churches and Religions in the Modern World A.D. 1900–2000* (Nairobi, Kenya: Oxford University Press, 1982), 3.
3. Ibid., 15.

4. C. Peter Wagner, *On the Crest of the Wave* (Ventura, Cal.: Regal Books, 1983), 9.
5. Ibid., 20–21.
6. Barrett, 3.
7. Ibid.
8. Ibid.
9. Ibid.
10. Quoted in Wagner, 25.
11. Ibid., 28.
12. Ibid., 12. Also see Phil Parshall, *Beyond the Mosque: Christians within Muslim Community* (Grand Rapids: Baker, 1985).
13. Keeley, 17, 22.
14. Sharon Mumper, "How to Start a Church in 50,000 Indonesian Villages," *Christianity Today,* Sept. 20, 1985, 42–44.
15. "Colombia Is Witnessing a Major Religious Revival," *Christianity Today,* Sept. 20, 1985, 40.
16. Ibid.
17. Ibid.
18. San Francisco (UPI): "Church Membership in Russia Growing," *Jackson [Michigan] Citizen Patriot,* Dec. 14, 1985, A–4.
19. Ibid.
20. Waldron Scott, "Evangelicals at a Crossroads," in Keeley, 108.
21. Wagner, 171.
22. Scott, in Keeley, 109.
23. Wagner, 10.
24. Ibid., 11.
25. Ibid., 154–55.
26. Ibid., 9.
27. Keeley, 80.
28. Ibid.
29. See Lyle Schaller, *Understanding Tomorrow* (Nashville: Abingdon, 1976), 66ff.
30. Naisbitt, 232.
31. Ibid., 246–47.

Chapter 2

1. George Gallup, Jr., "The Latest Trends in American Religion," *Christian Herald,* November 1982, 21.

2. Ibid.
3. Donald E. Hoke, ed., *Evangelicals Face the Future* (South Pasadena: The William Carey Library, 1978), 31.
4. Ibid., 32.
5. Ibid., 31.
6. Joseph Bayly, "The End of an Era," *Eternity,* October 1985, 79.
7. William J. Abraham, *The Coming Great Revival: Recovering the Full Evangelical Tradition* (San Francisco: Harper & Row, 1984), 112. Similarly, see Jeremy Rifkin, *The Emerging Order: God in the Age of Scarcity* (New York: G. P. Putman's Sons, 1979).
8. Russell P. Spittler, "Children of the Twentieth Century," in Keeley, 77.
9. Charles E. Hummel, *Fire in the Fireplace: Contemporary Charismatic Renewal* (Downers Grove: InterVarsity Press, 1978), 17–18.
10. Vinson Synan, *In the Latter Days: The Outpouring of the Holy Spirit in the Twentieth Century* (Ann Arbor: Servant Books, 1984), 7.
11. Ibid.
12. Ibid., 136.
13. Quoted in Synan, 136.
14. Robert E. Webber, *Evangelicals on the Canterbury Trail: Why Evangelicals Are Attracted to the Liturgical Church* (Waco: Word, 1985), 8.
15. Ibid., 15.
16. Ibid., 167.
17. Thomas Howard, *Evangelical Is Not Enough* (Nashville: Thomas Nelson, 1984), 149. See also Robert Webber and Donald Bloesch, eds., *The Orthodox Evangelicals* (Nashville: Thomas Nelson, 1978).
18. David L. McKenna, "In the World," *United Evangelical Action,* Nov./Dec. 1985.
19. Theodore Runyon, ed., *What the Spirit Is Saying to the Churches* (New York: Hawthorn Books, 1975), 107–108.
20. "Jerry Falwell's Crusade," *Time,* Sept. 2, 1985, 52.
21. Ibid.
22. *Christian Herald,* November 1982, 26.
23. Ibid.

24. Thomas Stransky, "Roman Catholics since the Council," in Keeley, 41–42.
25. "Taking Charge," *Jackson [Michigan] Citizen Patriot,* Jan 4. 1986, A–4.
26. Urbana, Md. (UPI), "Married Deacon Runs Parish without a Priest," *Jackson [Michigan] Citizen Patriot,* Jan. 5, 1986, B–7.
27. Ibid.
28. George Gallup and David Poling, *The Search for America's Faith* (Nashville: Abingdon, 1980), 57.
29. Bayly, 79.
30. UPI Wire Service, "Pope, Lutheran Leaders Pledge Closer Church Ties," *Jackson [Michigan] Citizen Patriot,* Sept. 27, 1985, A–12.
31. Ibid.
32. *Time,* March 17, 1986, 71.
33. James Hunter, *American Evangelicalism* (New Brunswick, N.J.: Rutgers University Press, 1983), 87, referring to the time since 1942 and the NAE.
34. Ibid.
35. See Bernard Semmel, *The Methodist Revolution* (New York: Basic Books, 1973).

Chapter 3

1. Fox Butterfield, *China: Alive in the Bitter Sea* (New York: Times Books, 1982), 7, 8. Quoted in G. Thompson Brown, *Christianity in the People's Republic of China* (Atlanta: John Knox Press, 1983), 178.
2. Brown, 177.
3. James H. Taylor, "Church Alive in China," from a 1985 address, Overseas Missionary Fellowship conference, Swanwick, England.
4. Jay and Linda Adams, *One Billion: A China Chronicle* (New York: Ballantine Books, 1983), 4–5.
5. Ibid.
6. Ibid., 19.
7. Tom Goosmann and Edward Plowman, "Visitors See Signs of Strong Evangelical Faith in China," *Christianity Today,* Sept. 6, 1985, 46.

8. Ibid.
9. Ibid., 46–48, and "What Is God Doing through the Church in China?" *Christianity Today,* Oct. 18, 1985, 47.
10. From an interview with Sam Wolgemuth in "What Is God Doing through the Church in China?" *Christianity Today,* Oct. 18, 1985, 48.
11. Ibid.
12. Keeley, 169.
13. Taylor, "Church Alive in China."
14. Keeley, 169.
15. Brown, 172.
16. See, for example, Howard A. Snyder, *The Radical Wesley and Patterns for Church Renewal* (Downers Grove: InterVarsity, 1980), 129–42.
17. Taylor, "Church Alive in China."
18. Brown, 172.
19. Taylor, "Church Alive in China."
20. Brown, 179.
21. Ibid., 179–180.
22. Taylor, "Church Alive in China."
23. Keeley, 167.
24. Ibid., 170.
25. Robert N. Bellah, et al., *Habits of the Heart: Individualism and Commitment in American Life* (Berkeley: University of California Press, 1985).
26. Quoted in Brown, 185; cf. 181–82.

Chapter 4

1. Naisbitt, 17.
2. Ibid., 75.
3. Ibid., 88.
4. Ibid., 85–86.
5. Natalie Angier, "Hanging the Universe on Strings," *Time,* Jan. 13, 1986, 56–57.
6. A few representative books are: Isaac C. Rottenberg, *The Promise and the Presence: Toward a Theology of the Kingdom of God* (Grand Rapids: Eerdmans, 1980); Robert H. Henderson, *Joy to the World: An Introduction to Kingdom Evan-*

gelism (Atlanta: John Knox Press, 1980); Lesslie Newbigin, *Sign of the Kingdom* (Grand Rapids: Eerdmans, 1980); Donald B. Kraybill, *The Upside-Down Kingdom* (Scottdale, Penn.: Herald Press, 1978); Peter Toon, *God's Kingdom for Today* (Westchester, Ill.: Cornerstone Books, 1980); Mortimer Arias, *Announcing the Reign of God* (Philadelphia: Fortress Press, 1984); Andrew J. Kirk, *Good News of the Kingdom Coming* (Downers Grove: InterVarsity, 1985); Howard A. Snyder, *A Kingdom Manifesto* (Downers Grove: InterVarsity, 1985); Pat Robertson, *The Secret Kingdom* (Nashville: Thomas Nelson, 1982). Books which have been seminally influential among some U.S. evangelicals include John Bright, *The Kingdom of God* (Nashville: Abingdon, 1953), Jacques Ellul, *The Presence of the Kingdom* (New York: Seabury, 1967), and the writings of George Eldon Ladd, including *Jesus and the Kingdom* (Waco: Word Books, 1964).

7. Richard F. Lovelace, "Thy Kingdom Come on Earth and in Heaven," unpublished manuscript, 1982.
8. John Bright, *The Kingdom of God*, 7.
9. C. Peter Wagner, *Church Growth and the Whole Gospel: A Biblical Mandate* (New York: Harper & Row, 1981), 3.
10. Naisbitt, 43.
11. Ibid., 36.
12. Ibid., 211.
13. Ibid., 212.
14. Ibid., 213.
15. Ibid., 213, 215, 221, 229.
16. Ibid., 228.
17. Ibid., 159, 188.
18. Gene Getz, *Sharpening the Focus of the Church* (Wheaton: Victor Books, 1984), 15–24.
19. Albert O. Hirschman, *Getting Ahead Collectively* (New York: Pergamon Press, 1984), 15–16.
20. Ibid., 100.
21. Ibid., 99.
22. Guillermo (William) Cook in *The Expectation of the Poor: Latin American Base Ecclesial Communities in Protestant Perspective* (Maryknoll, N.Y.: Orbis Books, 1985).

Chapter 5

1. Bruce Stabbert, *The Team Concept: Paul's Church Leadership Patterns or Ours?* (Tacoma, Washington: Hegg Bros. Printing, 1982).
2. Andrew Greeley, *Religion in the Year 2000* (New York: Sheed and Ward, 1969), 169–70.
3. Based on ideas suggested by Dr. Wesley Pinkham.
4. C. Peter Wagner, *Your Church Can Grow* (Glendale, Cal.: Regal Books, 1976), 57.
5. Ibid., 55.
6. Ibid., 65, 59.
7. These matters are dealt with more fully in earlier books by Howard A. Snyder: *The Community of the King* (InterVarsity, 1977), 73–96; *The Problem of Wineskins* (InterVarsity, 1975), chapter ten; and *Liberating the Church* (InterVarsity, 1983), especially chapter eight.
8. Philip Jacob Spener, *Pia Desideria*, ed. and trans. by Theodore Tappert (Philadelphia: Fortress Press, 1964), 92–93.

Chapter 6

1. Judith L. Weidman, ed., *Women Ministers* (San Francisco: Harper and Row, 1981, 1985), 3.
2. Ibid., 1–2.
3. Cf. Donald W. Dayton, *Discovering an Evangelical Heritage* (New York: Harper & Row, 1976).
4. George Marsden, *Fundamentalism and American Culture* (New York: Oxford, 1980), 83.
5. Marsden, 250–51; Howard A. Snyder, *Liberating the Church: The Ecology of Church and Kingdom* (Downers Grove: InterVarsity, 1983), 224ff.
6. B. T. Roberts, *Ordaining Women* (Rochester, N.Y.: Earnest Christian, 1891), 10.
7. Timothy L. Smith, *Called Unto Holiness: The Story of the Nazarenes: The Formative Years* (Kansas City, Mo.: Nazarene Publishing House, 1962), 155.
8. On women in missions, see Ruth A. Tucker, *From Jerusalem to Irian Jaya: A Biographical History of Christian Missions* (Grand Rapids: Zondervan, 1983).

9. Max Weber, *The Sociology of Religion*, trans. E. Fischoff (Boston: Beacon Press, 1963), 104.
10. Weidman, *Women Ministers* (1981 ed.), 4.
11. Marsden, 249–50.
12. *Time*, Sept. 2, 1985, 57.
13. Weidman (1981 ed.), 2.
14. George Barna and William McKay, *Vital Signs: Emerging Social Trends and the Future of American Christianity* (Westchester, Ill.: Crossway Books, 1984), 129.
15. Walter Liefeld and Ruth Tucker, *Women and the Church: A History of Changing Perspectives* (Grand Rapids, Michigan: Zondervan, 1986). [Quoted from pre-publication copy of chapter 10, "Modern Pentecostalism and Denominationalism: Tent-toting Evangelists and Ordained Ministers."]
16. Study reported in Fuller Theological Seminary's *Theology, News and Notes*, 32:3, Oct. 1985, 5–6; *Fact Book on Theological Education 1985–86*, Association of Theological Schools in the United States and Canada, 8–12.
17. *Fact Book 1985–86*, 8.
18. Statistics from personal interviews and correspondence.
19. Barna and McKay, 128.
20. Ibid.
21. *San José Mercury News* (Knight Ridder News Service), May 1985, reported in *Theology, News and Notes*, 32:3, Oct. 1985, 6; Barna and McKay, 129.
22. O. John Eldred, *Women Pastors* (Valley Forge, Pa.: Judson Press, 1981), 37.
23. Quoted in Liefeld and Tucker.
24. Leon McBeth, *Women in Baptist Life* (Nashville: Broadman, 1979), 153, quoted in Liefeld and Tucker.
25. Barna and McKay, 129.
26. Ibid., 130.
27. Eldred, 19.
28. Jackson W. Carroll, Barbara Hargrove, and Adair T. Lummis, *Women of the Cloth: A New Opportunity for the Churches* (San Francisco: Harper & Row, 1981), 156.
29. Bertil E. Gärtner and Carl Strandberg, "The Experience of the Church of Sweden," in Peter Moore, ed., *Man, Woman, and Priesthood* (London: SPCK, 1978), 123–33.
30. Weidman (1985 ed.), 8.

31. Rosemary Ruether and Eleanor McLaughlin, eds., *Women of Spirit* (New York: Simon and Schuster, 1979), 28.
32. Letty Russell, "Clerical Ministry as a Female Profession," *The Christian Century,* Feb. 7–14, 1979, 125–26.
33. Weidman (1985 ed.), 6, reporting a D. Min. study by Susan Murch Morrison, Wesley Theological Seminary, 1979.

Chapter 7

1. David Lyon, "The Secular Outlook Today," in Keeley, 25.
2. Barna and McKay, 136.
3. Ibid., 141.
4. Ibid.
5. Ibid., 143.
6. See "Who is the client" in Lyle Schaller, *Understanding Tomorrow* (Nashville: Abingdon, 1976), 91–93.
7. James Hunter, *American Evangelicalism* (New Brunswick, N.J.: Rutgers University Press, 1983), 97.
8. Kenneth Vaux, "How Do I Love Me?" *Christianity Today,* Sep. 20, 1985, 25.
9. John Bright, *The Kingdom of God*, 120.
10. Paul Johnson (author of *Modern Times*), "Why I Must Believe In God," *Reader's Digest,* June 1985, 126.
11. "The Latest Trends in American Religion," *Christian Herald,* Nov. 1982, 21.
12. Ibid., 24–26.
13. This is a composite, somewhat fictionalized account.
14. Boston (UPI), "Unselfish Trend: Officials say new collegians drifting away from 'me' attitudes of the yuppies," *Jackson* [*Michigan*] *Citizen Patriot,* Sept. 25, 1985.
15. Barna and McKay, 37, data from American Resource Bureau, Wheaton, Ill.
16. John Shelby Spong, *The Easter Moment,* quoted in "The Latest Trends in American Religion," *Christian Herald,* Nov. 1982, 26.
17. Ibid., 22–24.
18. *Light and Life,* April 1986, 27–28.
19. Naisbitt, 260.

Chapter 8

1. Naisbitt, 233.
2. George Masnik and Mary Jo Bane, *The Nation's Families: 1960–1990* (Boston: Joint Center for Urban Studies of MIT and Harvard University, 1980), 19, 9.
3. Ibid., 261, 264.
4. Ibid., 233.
5. Ibid., 233–34.
6. Masnick and Bane, 21.
7. *Time,* Sept. 2, 1985, 49–50.
8. Ibid., 50.
9. Schaller, 17.
10. Ibid.
11. Ibid., 17–20.
12. Kelly Kolhagen, Booth News Service, *Jackson [Michigan] Citizen Patriot,* Sept. 28, 1985, A–4.
13. Ibid.
14. Mei-Mei Chan, "Family: Still where the Heart Is," *USA Weekend,* Jan. 3–5, 1986, 4.
15. Ibid.

Chapter 9

1. "Jerry Falwell's Crusade," *Time,* Sept. 2, 1985.
2. Ibid.
3. Ibid.
4. Ibid., 52.
5. Virginia Beach, Va. (UPI) "Preacher for President? Giggles fading," *Jackson [Michigan] Citizen Patriot,* Jan. 12, 1986, A–3. Operation Blessing has been embroiled in some controversy for allegedly providing some support to the Contras in Nicaragua.
6. Washington (UPI) "Falwell Starts New Group," *Jackson [Michigan] Citizen Patriot,* Jan. 4, 1986, A–3.
7. *Time,* Sept. 2, 1985, 52.
8. Barna and McKay, 95.
9. Ibid., 96.
10. Schaller, 136.
11. For an elaboration of this ecological perspective from the standpoint of Scripture and the Christian faith, see Howard A.

Snyder, *Liberating the Church: The Ecology of Church and Kingdom* (Downers Grove: InterVarsity, 1983), 37–73.
12. "The Entrepreneurial Mystique," *Inc.*, Oct. 1985, 56.
13. Norman Geisler, "A Premillennial View of Law and Government," *Moody Monthly*, Oct. 1985, 129.
14. W. T. Purkiser, ed., *Exploring Our Christian Faith* (Kansas City, Mo.: Beacon Hill Press, 1960), 528–29.
15. Geisler, 129–131.
16. Stephen Mott, *Biblical Ethics and Social Change* (New York: Oxford University Press, 1984).
17. Schaller, 23–31.
18. Naisbitt, 116, 103.
19. Ibid., 121, 124.
20. Schaller, 85.
21. John Briggs, "The Global Village," in Keeley, 20.

Chapter 10

1. Herman Kahn, *World Economic Development: 1979 and Beyond* (New York: Morrow Quill Paperbacks, 1979), 61.
2. Ibid., 62.
3. Ibid., 60–61.
4. Ibid., 64.
5. Ibid., 64, 65.
6. Ibid., 69.
7. John Briggs, "The Global Village," in Keeley, p. 21.
8. "Karl Menninger Analyzes World, Finds That It's in Need of Help," *The Wall Street Journal*, Dec. 23, 1985, 1. See Ronald J. Sider and Richard K. Taylor, *Nuclear Holocaust and Christian Hope: A Book for Christian Peacemakers* (Downers Grove: InterVarsity Press, 1982). Actually, Sider and Taylor call for effective Christian action, not passive waiting for God's intervention.
9. Barbara W. Tuchman, *A Distant Mirror: The Calamitous 14th Century* (New York: Alfred A. Knopf, 1978).

Conclusion

1. Donald E. Hoke, ed., *Evangelicals Face the Future* (South Pasadena: The William Carey Library, 1978), 29–30.
2. Bertram Gross, *Friendly Fascism: The New Face of Power in America* (New York: M. Evans and Company, 1980), 3.